MENTAL GYMNASTICS

For Trivia Freaks and Puzzle Nuts

MENTAL GYMNASTICS

For Trivia Freaks and Puzzle Nuts

KEN WEBER

Second printing in 1989 by
Stoddart Publishing Co. Limited
34 Lesmill Road
Toronto, Canada
M3B 2T6

Published in 1984 by Methuen Publications

CANADIAN CATALOGUING IN PUBLICATION DATA

Weber, K.J. (Kenneth Jerome), 1940-
Mental gymnastics for trivia freaks and puzzle nuts

ISBN 0-7737-5322-2

1. Puzzles. 2. Questions and answers.
I. Title.

GV1493.W4 1989 793.73 C89-094397-4

Design: Brant Cowie/ArtPlus Limited
Cover Illustration: Sherban S. Valentin

Printed in Canada

MENTAL GYMNASTICS

For Trivia Freaks and Puzzle Nuts

Trifles and Tangents

Oh Yes! Good Old What's His Name!

Singer Steve Lawrence might never have made it under his real name, Sidney Leibowitz. And would you applaud David Kaminsky as easily as you applaud Danny Kaye? In a way you can't blame them for seeking out names that are easier on the English-speaking tongue. Sometimes it was almost necessary. Diana Dors, for example, was born Diana Fluck. And could you imagine American audiences trying to pronounce Gwyllyn Ford instead of Glenn Ford? Then there were those who went the other way. H.G. Wells (his real name) once published under the name of Walker Glockenhammer!

The names that follow are all real ones (with one exception—find it!) from the not-so-distant past. They are also names you probably remember. The key is: *Why* do you remember them? Why should you know them?

1. James Meredith
2. Margaret Sinclair
3. James W. McCord
4. Bessie Wallis Warfield
5. Edward Brooke
6. Clifford Irving
7. Richard Starkey
8. Allan Dafoe
9. Amanda Blake
10. Valentina Tereshkova
11. Francis Chichester
12. Florence Chadwick
13. Martha Mitchell
14. James Cross
15. Bill Barilko
16. Felix Leiter
17. Ferhat Abbas
18. Odumegwu Ojukwu (Lieut.-Colonel)

visuthink

You have seen these before.

once lightly	g o s s i p	wave radio	c a p t a i n	noon good	bathing suit

And you probably had no trouble getting "once over lightly," "gossip column," "shortwave radio," "Captain Hook," "good afternoon," and "topless bathing suit."

1. These may be a slightly greater problem.

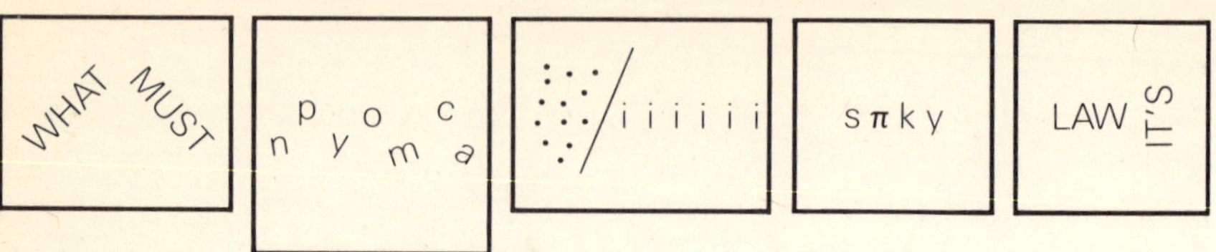

2. These are even harder.

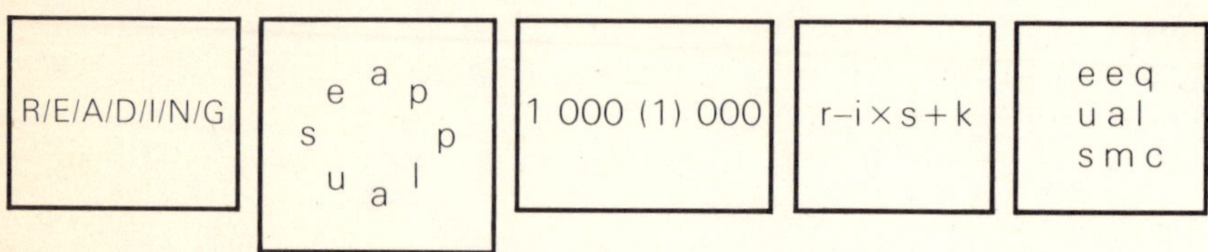

3. And if you can get these, you're really something!

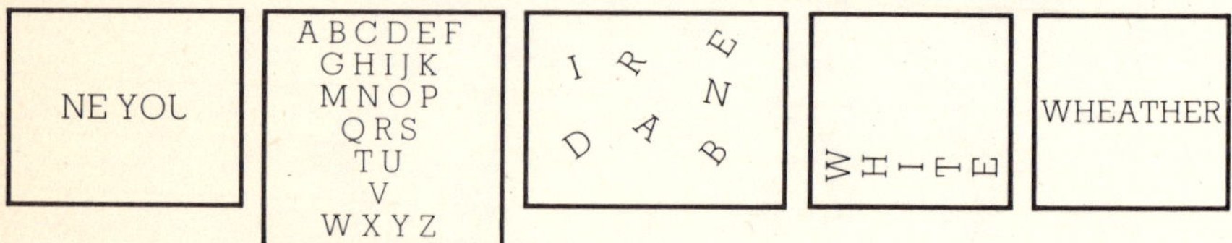

SHERLOCK of the John

The Case of the Stolen Stamps

In the doorway of Mieke's office stood a very contrite and edgy Miles Mastrollo. In fact, as he waited for Mieke to acknowledge him, his fidgeting took him farther out of her office than in.

"Sit down, young man, for heaven's sake!" Mieke ordered without looking up. "If you're going to rotate, better wear out the chair than the rug."

Miles slanted across the floor to the only chair that was empty of books and files and all the other bits of flotsam that indicated a very busy office. He perched on the edge with his knees drawn up, heels off the floor.

"It didn't arrive. The shipment. Did it?" he ventured.

Mieke looked over the top of her glasses. "No it didn't," she sighed. "The first bonded shipment that Ninth Line Courier Service has ever failed to deliver. You have earned yourself a real distinction." Mieke was looking through her glasses now, and Miles' nervous spasms increased.

"And it shouldn't surprise you to learn," she continued, "that the stamp collection was worth almost half a million. That's why we always use a police escort for antiques and collectibles."

"I know that." Miles stopped moving around. "I know that. So how can you blame me if the cops stole it? I mean at least they looked like cops."

Mieke spread her hands on the desk. "OK. Let's go through it one more time. You say two policemen took the stamp collection. Just like that."

Miles reddened and began to squirm again. "Not just like that. It was all standard procedure. From here to the border, there was a Vancouver city police car in front and one in back of me. At the border we were met by the two motorcycle cops from Bellingham. There was no reason to be suspicious. Their bikes were real. So were their uniforms. They were real motorcycle cops. I mean—they looked like real ones. They had the boots and the gloves, and the sunglasses, and the white helmets."

Miles was becoming more confident now. As Mieke opened her mouth to speak, he continued.

"You'd have thought they were police too. I mean, they even *acted* like motorcycle cops. You know, sort of strutty and cocky and . . ."

"According to this report," interrupted Mieke, "you got a good look at one of them."

Miles took a deep breath. "Yea, when they stepped out on the highway and made me get out—that's when they took the van and left me there—the one that put his bike in the van and got in the driver's seat, he got pretty close."

"And according to your description," Mieke held up a file folder, "he is about a head taller than you, heavier; he's got blue eyes, and a reddish moustache."

"Yea, and a little nick on his right cheek. Like he maybe cut himself shaving," Miles added.

Mieke looked up from the folder. "And you say all this took place in a few seconds. They stopped. You stopped. You were ordered out of the van. They put one of the bikes in and drove away leaving you on the side of the road."

"Just like that," Miles responded. "I mean, are *you* going to argue when your escort—I mean, they're cops too—tells you to stop and get out?"

"Especially not if you're all on the same team," Mieke countered.

What made Mieke suspicious?

Contemplator's Corner

Relax. You don't need a pencil for these.

1. With one small stroke, you can make this a correct equation. (Putting a stroke through the equal sign, however, is strictly amateur.)

$$5 + 5 + 5 = 550$$

2. Translate this mathematical limerick into a true verbal limerick. (If you need a start, try "A dozen, a . . .")

$$\frac{12 + 144 + 20 + 3\sqrt{4}}{7} + 5(11) = 9^2 + 0$$

3. Half-frozen and near death from exposure, you stumble into the abandoned prospector's cabin. Clutching your one remaining match in your near-lifeless fingers, you survey the cabin and note a fireplace and a small stove, each filled with wood and ready to go, a kerosene heater, and a lantern. What do you light first?

4. What's the wrong number in this sequence?

100, 72, 36, 16, 4

IN A WORD

Expansion Graft

1. By adding the same letter of the alphabet to each of the four-letter words below, and then rearranging the letters, you can make five-letter words, each of which has the same letter in the third position.

   For example, if the special letter were *x* (it isn't), then by adding it to the four-letter words "into" and "robe," and rearranging, you could make the five-letter words "toxin" and "boxer." Give it a try.

tire ____ ____ [____] ____ ____
nail ____ ____ [____] ____ ____
core ____ ____ [____] ____ ____
hole ____ ____ [____] ____ ____
rile ____ ____ [____] ____ ____
ocha ____ ____ [____] ____ ____
soar ____ ____ [____] ____ ____
cone ____ ____ [____] ____ ____

2. Now to really test you, do the same exercise, except that this time you must add the same two-letter consonant blend to turn these four-letter words into six-letter words. The consonant blend is in the third and fourth positions each time.

reef ____ ____ [____ ____] ____ ____
blue ____ ____ [____ ____] ____ ____
hire ____ ____ [____ ____] ____ ____
lace ____ ____ [____ ____] ____ ____
roam ____ ____ [____ ____] ____ ____
alas ____ ____ [____ ____] ____ ____
bait ____ ____ [____ ____] ____ ____
over ____ ____ [____ ____] ____ ____

Trifles and Tangents

From Sunday Afternoon TV

In the latter half of the nineteenth century, the Duke of Beaufort rather enjoyed a game of "poona" on a Sunday afternoon. (What else was one to do in India?) But when he imported the game to England it just wouldn't do to call it "poona." Who, after all, would play "poona"? So he renamed it "badminton" after his estate in Somerset.

He had more flair than Dr. James Naismith, the Ontario-born inventor of basketball. He called it "indoor rugby" at first. But then, not everyone can deal fluently with sport. Can you?

1. Name at least eight games that are played with balls that are neither inflated nor hollow.
2. In what sport do the players getting the greatest number of points lose?
3. Had it not been for horses, this sport would never have developed. Yet for the entire game, the horses never leave the stable—usually. What sport?
4. What is the *least* number of pitches, in a baseball game, that the visiting team pitcher could throw in a losing game?
5. In 1936, the Olympic Games were held for the last time, before a long break. What year did they reopen?
6. What was unique about the World Series victory of Boston over Pittsburgh in 1903?
7. Since John L. Sullivan, the last bare-knuckle heavyweight boxing champion, there have been *five* title holders who were not from the United States. How many can you name?
8. Name, within two years, the year of the first game played in the National Hockey League.
9. For a nation with so much ice, Canada has won an Olympic gold medal for figure skating only once. When, and by whom?

10. What young woman in the 1970s held the record for the fastest ever swim across Lake Ontario, and a double crossing of the English Channel?

11. Curling's big international series is the Silver Broom. There have been two others, both a lot older. Can you name either of them?

12. The Walker Cup and the Curtis Cup both differ from the Ryder Cup. How?

13. In what sport would you
    a. pot winks?
    b. make a cradle cannon?
    c. make a two-handed dead left?
    d. play in a fronton?
    e. shoot a Portsmouth Round?

The "Such Wit" Graffiti Page

Humpty Dumpty
was pushed!

Amo amas
Amat it again!

Orville was
Wright!

1,000,000 lemmings
can't be wrong!

Existentialism has
no future

In the beginning was
the word. And the word
was "AARDVARK"

Oedipus was the first
to bridge the generation gap

All this stuff about sadism
necrophilia and bestiality
is just flogging a dead horse

Jack the Ripper is alive and working in our laundry

Planning Boards do it with their eyes shut

Power Corrupts. Absolute power is even more fun!

Reality is for people who can't cope with drugs

The trouble with political jokes is they get elected

Contemplator's Corner

Greenhouse Square

1. Just outside Leamington four flower growers leased greenhouses on the perimeter of a square field. On the northern edge, Jack Atkin raised geraniums. Ron Minaker leased a greenhouse to the immediate left of Ron Forrester. The greenhouse with the chrysanthemums is not Forrester's, and the one with the poinsettias is not the one leased to Bill Lacroix. Nevertheless, the Easter lilies are opposite the poinsettias.

   Whose greenhouses are where in this square field?

Cecile's Conundrum

2. If time is really dragging, you may need this one. First borrow some matches, or if an accountant is nearby, some pencils. Or depending where you are, some tongue depressors, or Q-Tips, or whatever. Use your imagination!

   You need 10. Arrange them like this:

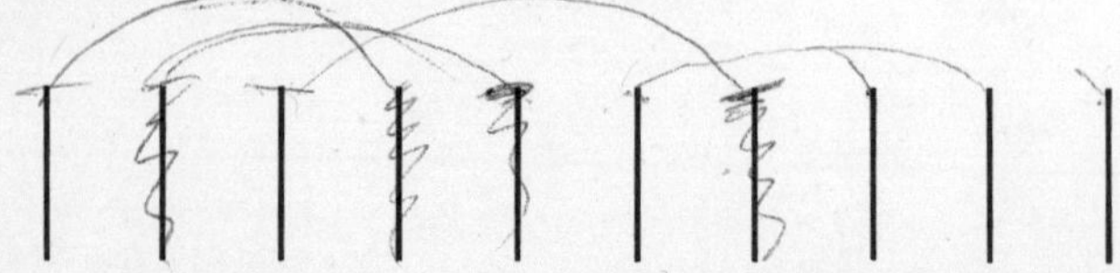

Now, the idea is to rearrange them so they are in T's like this.

BUT, you may only move in jumps. AND, you must jump *two* matches (or whatever) at a time. Any T that you form counts as two. This exercise can be accomplished in *five* jumps.

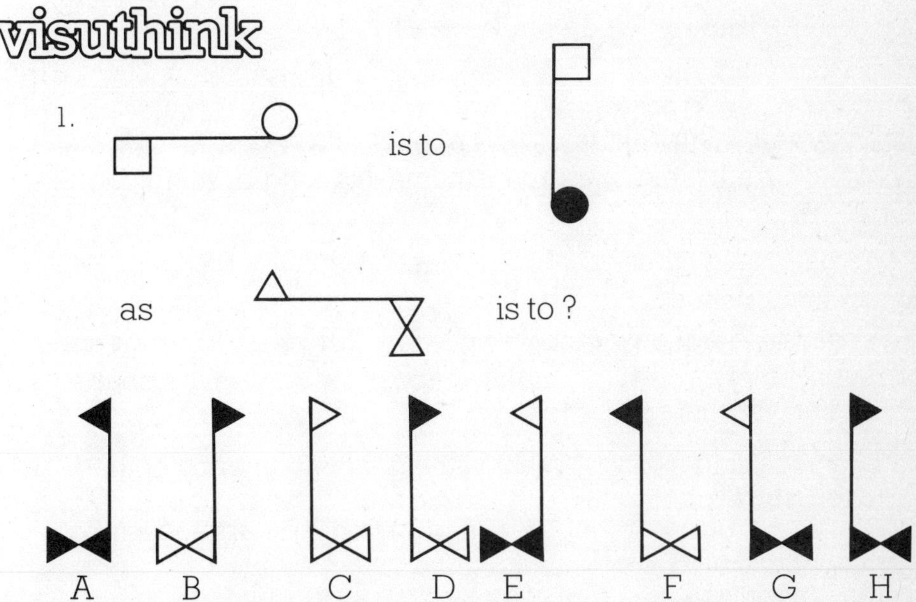

2. Which one is the odd one out?

Trifles and Tangents

Sing Me Another One

In the original working notes for "Old Folks at Home" (1851), Stephen Foster tried out "Way down upon the Yazoo River" (and even Pee Dee River) before he settled on Swanee. "How Dry I Am" was written to be a hymn, in 1891. "Carolina in the Morning" (1922) was written by Walter Donaldson before he was ever in Carolina, and "Take Me Out to the Ball Game" (1908)—you guessed it: composer Albert Von Tilzer didn't see a ball game until 1928.

1. What distinction does Elvis Presley's "Don't Be Cruel" share with Chubby Checker's "The Twist," Debbie Reynolds' "Tammy" and Patti Page's "Tennessee Waltz"?

2. "Frosty the Snowman" (1952), "Rudolph the Red-Nosed Reindeer" (1950) and "Here Comes Peter Cottontail" (1955) were all million sellers recorded by the same singer. Who? As a bonus, can you name his long-running radio show?

3. What band played "the sweetest music this side of heaven"?

4. A record by Bill Haley and His Comets became in 1953 the first rock 'n roll hit to make *Billboard's* best-seller charts. What was this song?

5. Famous sing-a-longs: What is the *next* line in each of these well-known classics?
   a. "Pack up your troubles in your old kit bag and smile, smile, smile"
   b. "My wild Irish rose, the sweetest flower that grows"
   c. "When whipoorwill come, and evening is nigh"
   d. "You bring along your Cadillac; leave my old wreck behind"
   e. "What would you think if I sang out of tune?"

6. This country and western singer holds the record for most consecutive years on the best-selling charts. Who? (His first million seller was "I'm Movin On" (1936).)

7. Even some members of the S.P.E.B.S.Q.S.A. (Society for the Preservation and Encouragement of Barbershop Quartet Singing in America) might have a mild struggle with these.

Match the name of the song with the opening line of the first *verse*. (Everybody knows the chorus.)

"Sweet Adeline," "Meet Me Tonight in Dreamland," "Wait 'Till the Sun Shines, Nellie," "My Gal Sal," "Let Me Call You Sweetheart."

a. "On a Sunday morn, sat a maid forlorn,
With her sweetheart by her side"

b. "In the evening when I sit alone a-dreaming,
Of days gone by, love, to me so dear"

c. "I am dreaming, dear, of you, day by day,"
Dreaming when the skies are blue; when they're gray"

d. "Everything is over, and I'm feeling bad.
I lost the best pal that I ever had"

e. "Dreaming of you. That's all I do.
Night and day, for you I'm pining"

IN A WORD

What's Missing?

When the blanks are filled with the correct words or letters in the two columns below, each pair of words, when read across, will be a common expression or well-known name or title. The first one, for example, is "pie shell." The fourth is a well-known British author. To help you, the missing words are listed at the side. There are a few extra and unneeded words in the list just to make it interesting. Missing letters are *your* problem.

1. p ie shell
2. ____dd __________
3. __________ ____mptiness
4. __________ ____augh
5. __________ ____ree
6. ____ying ____
7. ____aqui __________
8. __________ ____ast
9. ____nti- __________
10. __________ ____oll
11. e ven steven.

steven, nuclear,
Indians, window,
under, Middle,
shell, Evelyn,
running, Fellows,
elevator, book,
vast, run
kewpie,

Now, if you have done it right, the first letters reading down the left column, and the first reading down the right, should give you a well-known saying.

Contemplator's Corner

Puzzles without a Pencil

1. When the dormitory went co-ed, the elderly matron in charge arranged the beds so that if male and female students slept in beds side by side, the boys' heads were always pointed in the same direction as the girls' feet.

   If there were three heads pointing east in every room, and three pairs of feet pointing west, how many students were sleeping in each room?

2. Correct this equation. *No* pencil!

   XI + I = X

3. True or false: It is possible to make four 9's equal to 100.

4. How many letters of the alphabet can be written upside down?

SHERLOCK of the John

The Case of the Green Chev

Chief Gary Westlake backed his cruiser off the highway into a little cul-de-sac, and got out slowly. For what seemed like the hundredth time in the last hour he took off his hat and wiped the sweat band and then his face. In either direction the highway was shimmering in the heat, little waves that rose in the air and distorted any perspective one had of the distance. He couldn't remember a hotter day. Not the kind of day to look for bank robbers. Especially with the help he'd had from the witnesses.

A green Chev, they'd said, with a broken right headlight. On that part they had agreed. But after that the heat must have gotten to them. "They went north," said one. "Yes but they turned west," another insisted. And in front of the bank one had sworn they had gone south. Now here he was, having covered the four directions out of town, and there wasn't a trace.

Wearily he got back into the patrol car and pulled out into the shimmering waves toward town. He'd barely reached the speed limit when he saw the hitchhiker.

"Wow! Thanks!" The young man clambered into the front seat beside Chief Westlake. "I thought I was going to cook out there." He set a tattered backpack carefully between his legs, took a chocolate bar out of his shirt pocket, broke off a piece and offered it to the Chief. "I'm starved. You're the first car in this direction in almost an hour! Not much traffic the other way either."

"Didn't see any green cars going the other way did you?" Chief Westlake asked.

"Well I don't usually pay much attention, but there was this one, a Chev I think, with a headlight out. That's what made me notice. Don't remember which side though.

"Say can you drop me at the first restaurant?" the young man continued. "I'm really hungry."

"No, I don't think so," the Chief replied. "We've got some talking to do first."

What made Chief Westlake suspicious?

Trifles and Tangents

Pass the Oats

Shortly after George Washington had become comfortably ensconced as first president of the republic, he was presented a gift by the king of Spain. It was a jackass. The king certainly intended no offense, but obviously knew his politics.

Washington, incidentally, bred it to a stallion and produced a mule. It is the first *recorded* breeding of a mule in North America.

Mules, horses and even jackasses are not confined to governmental circles, however. You should be able to answer these horsey questions on the basis of general knowledge.

1. Hercules of Greek mythology was given a horse by Adrastus. It was called:
   a. Pegasus
   b. Denos
   c. Arion
   d. Castor

2. A horse is usually described as a certain number of *hands* high.
   A hand is: *a.* 3 inches
   b. 4 inches
   c. 5 inches
   d. 6 inches

   The measurement is taken at:
   a. the hind hoof to the top of the rump
   b. the fore hoof to the top of the shoulder
   c. the fore hoof to the top of the mane

3. The collective noun for *racehorses* is:
   a. sounder
   b. gate
   c. string
   d. muster

4. Match the horses and the owners

Gene Autry	Horse
Duke of Wellington	Brigham
El Cid	Babieca
Buffalo Bill Cody	Champion
Barney Google	Bucephalus

Tom Mix	Copenhagen
Tom Mix's first horse	Tony
Hopalong Cassidy	Spark Plug
Alexander the Great	Topper
Dudley Do-Right	Old Blue

5. Canada has won the Olympic gold medal in equestrian jumping at only one Olympiad. Which one and in what year?

6. True or false: Polo is played by two teams of *either* three or four horses and riders each.

7. *a.* Which two of these four stakes races are the same distance?
   Kentucky Derby
   Queen's Plate
   Preakness
   Belmont Stakes

   b. Only one winner of the Kentucky Derby has ever run it faster than Northern Dancer, the sole Canadian horse to win it, and that one winner had a Canadian jockey. Who was the jockey and on what horse?

Diverting Articles

Flushed with Ingenuity

1889. A year of enormous significance in the progress of humankind. The Eiffel Tower was completed in Paris. Pedro II of Brazil abdicated to permit a presidential republic. George Eastman produced rolled film for cameras. César Franck published his D minor symphony. And in Brighton, England, D.T. Bostel invented the washdown wooden water closet, thus closing the lid on centuries of discomfort and inconvenience for the most necessary of necessaries. Bostel's device was an inspired one that not only sprayed water over the sides of the toilet bowl after each use, but also allowed for water to remain in the bottom between uses. In fact, he might have become known as the father of the flush had it not been for an ingenious and considerably more entrepreneurial type, a Yorkshireman named Thomas Crapper.

Admittedly, Crapper's name alone was bound to win the recognition sweepstakes, for it obviously had a much greater phonetic appeal to aficionados of loo history. But he did indeed introduce a major invention: a mechanism that shut off the flow to the reservoir once it was filled. Prior to this, a user had to wait in the john until the tank had filled and then shut off the water flow manually. Not all that bad a prospect to a devoted bathroom reader, but many fastidious Victorians had adopted the habit of simply leaving the water running continuously, a practice that would cause apoplexy in modern-day waterworks engineers.

In any case, Crapper's salesmanship was bound to outdistance his peers. With his advertising campaign:

> Crapper's Valveless Waste Preventer
> Certain Flush With Easy Pull

and

> Crapper's Cedar Wood Seats Have The
> Advantage Of Being Warm . . . And Subtlely Aromatic

his name soon became synonymous with the WC. And if there were any need to guarantee his fame, it came when he won the biffy contract for Queen Victoria's castle at Sandringham. Thirty separate units were required to fulfill the royal needs, and Crapper did the job well enough to earn four royal warrants. Thus, "By Appointment To Her Majesty the Queen" appeared beside the claims for easy pull and aromatic seats.

Today's refinements to bathroom comfort are limited only to the inventive genius of marketing. For the right amount of money you can indent a slab of soft plastic with your posterior, air freight this mold to Italy, and receive in due course your personalized toilet seat fit to your shape, all in the glory of Italian marble. For a slightly higher cost, you can add electronic switches to the seat that will bring in prerecorded music. Each switch, incidentally, can be adjusted to respond to weight so that the personal musical tastes of all users will be met as they settle gently into position. By comparison, such luxury makes Crapper's deluxe models (The Cascade, The Deluge, The Niagara) seem a trifle naive. But despite the unlimited indulgence made possible by modern technology, it is Crapper who will live on as the true hero of the john—he, and the unsung Bostel.

ICE-BREAKERS

Inside Information that is Bound To Impress

Former president Richard M. Nixon is a ninth cousin to Leka I, exiled king of Albania. (*Burke's Royal Families of the World.*)

Judas Iscariot had red hair.

Albert Einstein changed his citizenship five times. (German b. 1894; stateless to 1897; Swiss to 1910; Austro-Hungarian to 1918; German to 1936; American until his death.)

Thomas Adams, the photographer who developed chewing gum, first proposed it as a substitute for rubber.

Mel Blanc is allergic to carrots.

J. Edgar Hoover would never allow anyone to step on his shadow, and one of the duties of his immediate staff was to see that this never happened.

Rin Tin Tin died in 1932 in Jean Harlow's arms.

A young Gregory Peck can be seen in the men's clothing pages of the 1940 Montgomery Ward catalogue.

The Museum of Modern Art in New York hung Matisse's *Le Bateau* upside down for 47 days before the error was discovered.

Bob Hope once tried a career as a boxer, using the name Packy Ease.

In Providence, Rhode Island, Stanley Pinto, a professional wrestler, in the opening minutes of a serious match—this was not a fix—entangled himself in the ropes. In his attempts to struggle free, he pinned his own shoulders to the floor for three seconds and lost the bout.

Long before Erich Von Daniken wrote *Chariots of the Gods*, he had been tried in court for fraud.

It cannot be proven from the New Testament that Jesus ever smiled.

In a response to traffic congestion, the government of Rome, under Julius Caesar, banned all wheeled vehicles from the heart of the city during daylight hours.

Contemplator's Corner

1. You have three colors to shade in the squares of this grid. Three squares must be puce, three ochre and three vermilion. But no two squares of the same color may be in the same row or column.

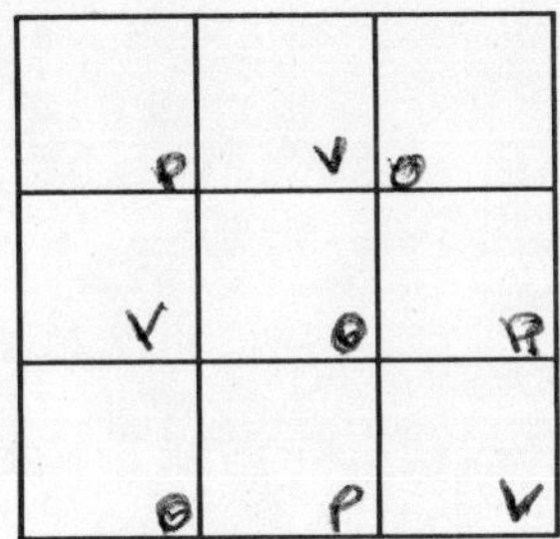

2. This time the grid is larger, so a switch to numbers is appropriate. Use the digits 1, 2, 3, 4, 5, and no others. Enter them so that no number is repeated in a row, or a column, or a diagonal. Naturally you must fill every square.

1	2	3	4	5

3. For variety, switch to the numbers 1 to 8 inclusive. Arrange them in the grid so that each number appears *once*, and no *consecutive* numbers are adjacent horizontally, vertically or diagonally.

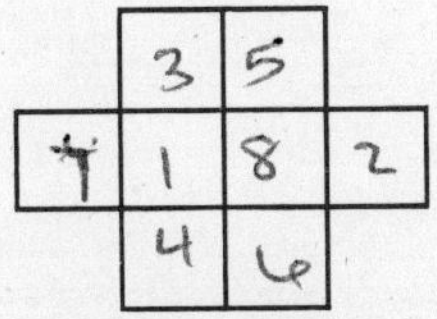

Trifles and Tangents

Who Was That Again?

If someone asked you if you remember Effie Klinker and Podine Puffington, you'd probably take a minute to realize that they were on the Edgar Bergen show with Charlie McCarthy and Mortimer Snerd. And unless you are really into football, it would probably take more than a minute to come up with the name of the first Heisman Trophy winner (Jay Berwanger in 1935; he was also the first to be drafted by an NFL team: Philadelphia in 1936). These names, however, should be a good deal easier.

1. This person moved Dwight D. Eisenhower's election campaign off the front pages several times in 1952. He was a former GI who went to Denmark for a series of operations and hormone injections. When she came back, she was famous. Who?

2. According to legend, in 490 BC he ran from Marathon to Athens (about 26 miles) to announce the Persians had been defeated. Who?

3. This act appeared more times on *The Ed Sullivan Show* than any other single act in its history. Do you have any names?

4. These two became famous—and remained so—after it was discovered in 1963 that members of the British establishment and the NKVD were alternating in their beds. They brought down the Tory government that year. Can you name both of them?

5. His pet on the TV show was named Flub-a-Dub, and he had companions like Princess Summerfallwinter-spring and Cornelius J. Cobb. His name?

6. This fictional character was Throckmorton P. ______, bachelor uncle of Marjorie and Leroy, and friend to Floyd the barber, Judge Hooker and many other memorable characters like Peavey the druggist. Throckmorton P. who?

7. This lady was inducted into the Swimming Pool Hall of Fame in 1967, not for her swimming pool company, which went broke, but for her movies in the '40s and '50s. (She wasn't inducted for her acting either!) Who was this terrific swimmer who looked so great in the water?

8. For running the British war material program so well in World War II, this Canadian became Lord Beaverbrook. What is his "common" name?

9. This young lady wowed the world at the 1976 Olympics in Montreal. She attained the first-ever perfect score in gymnastics. Her name?

10. Camp X, the graduate-level spy school for the Allies in World War II, was very quietly run outside Whitby, Ontario, by this man.

11. In the spring of 1925, this mathematics teacher read his students a portion of Hunter's *Civic Biology*. Dayton, Tennessee, was not ready for the theories of evolution. Who was he?

12. The world held its breath in August 1968 for this man who had led Czechoslovakia through its "springtime of freedom" and was now watching Russian tanks roll through Prague. Who was this Czech leader?

Invitational Graffiti

(irresistible responses to unwilling signs and slogans)

Please do not flush while train is standing at the station

(Except in Brantford)

Brigham's Tool Works

So?

Free Quebec!

In every package

Where will *you* be on Judgment Day?

Right here still waiting for the damn bus

Join the army! Visit exciting places!

Then destroy them!

Be a volunteer Blood Donor!

(That's the best Kind)

What will you do when Jesus comes?

Move Gretzky to right wing.

Thursday's Topic: How Labor Unions Succeed

On Friday: How To Nail Jelly To The Ceiling

Nine out of ten doctors prefer Camels!

And the tenth finds sheep irresistible

Every day four trains leave for Windsor

and then disappear off the face of the earth

The cremation of Mr. __________ will take place at 2 p.m. in St. James

Can you put him on low? I can't get there till 4:30

The Case of the Strange Suicide

Inspector Nicholson braked hard as he pulled up in front of the big office building. Ahead of him a patrol car sat flashing its red message. The white door stood open, an indication of how fast the driver had responded to the emergency call.

Nicholson pressed through the crowd that had gathered on the sidewalk. There is nothing to see, he said to himself, but crowds gather anyway. All you need to do is turn on your red light and you've got people all over the place. And they all want to see blood too!

"They're up there!" a doorman was shouting at him.

"Who's up there?" Nicholson wanted to know.

"Your uniformed man, and the guy who turned in the alarm! He saw it all y'know! He saw the guy kill himself!" The doorman was very excited.

Nicholson looked around the lobby. "Where's the elevator?" he asked.

"It's broken!" the doorman said. "You'll have to use the stairs. Fourth floor. The door's right over there."

Inspector Nicholson was puffing by the time he made it up to the murder scene. The patrolman was standing in the doorway with a tall man in a chauffeur's uniform.

"Right this way, Inspector!" said the patrolman. "The body's still there. We haven't touched a thing." He pointed to the chauffeur. "This man is a witness. Saw the guy hang himself."

The office was big. And it was rich. The furniture was expensive, the rug was thick. There was a well-stocked bar set into one wall. In fact, Nicholson thought, the only thing wrong was the body of a middle-aged man, a rope around his neck, hanging from a beam in the ceiling. Beneath him, an upturned footstool lay on the rug.

Nicholson walked over to the window, pulled the drapes and looked out. The crowd was still there and getting larger. Two more police cars had come in and added to the excitement. He turned to the chauffeur.

"You're the witness, eh? Do you know the dead man?"

"Well sure. He's—was—my boss! I was coming to pick him up. That's the limousine out in front. The gray one."

Inspector Nicholson looked at him carefully. "Tell us what happened."

"Well, I just pulled up in front and got out. The boss always limped a bit, see, and I was going to help him down the stairs. When I got out of the car, I looked up. I always do 'cause sometimes he waits on the balcony. He gets mad if I'm late. Anyway, I looked up, see, and there he is getting on that footstool with the rope around his neck. And I know he's going to kill himself, see, but with the elevator broken, by the time I ran up four floors, he was already dead, see?"

"Yes, I see," said Nicholson. "I think you'd better come with me. You've got more to tell us."

What made Inspector Nicholson suspicious?

ICE-BREAKERS

More Things You Have To Know

In 1922, Wallace J. Murray of Gorham, Maine, made a silk purse out of a sow's ear. It can be seen at the Smithsonian Institution in Washington, D.C.

In 1954–5, Ghia of Italy developed an experimental car for Chrysler. The $100,000 vehicle went down on the *Andrea Doria* on its way to America.

Canada's first association of prostitutes was called BEAVER (Better End All Vicious, Erotic Repression). The American association COYOTE stands for Call Off Your Old Tired Ethics.

Among the most trusting fools of all time was Joseph T. Grant, who challenged Billy the Kid to a gunfight at Fort Sumner, New Mexico, on January 24, 1880. Billy asked to check Grant's gun and secretly adjusted it so that it would fire the next shot on an empty chamber. Grant apparently did not check it again when it was returned to him. In Hargrove's saloon, where the fight took place, Billy the Kid won—for obvious reasons.

Tom Longboat (1887–1949), one of Canada's foremost runners, outran a horse over a twelve-mile course in 1906. The following year he won the Boston Marathon in a record time.

The first Miss America (Margaret Gorman in 1921) measured 30-25-32.

Lady Gough's *Book of Etiquette*, published near the end of Victoria's reign, proscribed the shelving of books by male authors beside those of female authors unless, of course, the authors were married.

Pete Gray was the only one-armed outfielder ever to play major league baseball. In 1945 he played for the old St. Louis Browns, batting .218. (He was missing his right arm. Also, his real name was Peter Wyshner.)

Trifles and Tangents

Getting There is Half the Fun

Chinese Gordon (Charles George Gordon, 1833–1885, also known as Gordon Pasha) held out at Khartoum against the Mahdi's forces for ten months while the British government diddled about whether, and when, and how, to relieve him. When the decision was finally taken, the War Department hired Thomas Cook & Son, the travel agency, to arrange the expedition. The expedition used a total of 1,505 vessels, from ocean liners to whaleboats. And it arrived too late.

Before you blame the travel agent—or anyone, try your own hand at this geography.

In what *country* would you be if:

1. you were in the city of Tripoli?
2. the Atlantic Ocean is west of the Pacific?
3. you were in the northernmost part of Scandinavia?
4. the national flag is not four-sided?
5. the Dominican Republic was in the other half of this island?
6. the four official languages are German, Italian, French, and Romansh?
7. some of the mountains in this country's Alps are named Koskiusko, Jagangul, Bogong, Feathertop?
8. the capital city is Bucharest?
9. it contains the only Great Lake entirely within its borders?
10. the border touches every other country on the continent, but two?
11. you were standing on the north magnetic pole?

IN A WORD

Ten into Six

Each definition here describes a six-letter word that has the number *ten* in it, as in LISTEN, for example, or MITTEN.

1. You can play singles or doubles.
2. soft and warm and gentle
3. They are usually a cuter animal at this stage.
4. a plan or purpose
5. It violates one of the senses.
6. You may do this in fear, or in embarrassment.
7. to be present
8. foul and spoiled
9. to speed along
10. a guarantee of position
11. defeated
12. a renter

visuthink

Cubing without the Rubik Strain

The one thing you *don't* do in the solution of this problem is draw anything. It would spoil the fun. You must envision the images here, and then respond from the picture in your head.

Lying before you is a large pile of identical wooden cubes. They are all painted white on all sides, and each measures one centimeter along any side.

1. How many of these smaller cubes would it take to build a larger one measuring 4 cm?

2. How many corners does the large cube have? Are there more or fewer flat sides to this large cube than there are corners?

3. Quickly now, if you were to measure all the edges of this large cube, their total linear length would be 16? 32? 48? 64?

4. Now remove one quarter of the large cube and imagine that the new cube has been painted blue on all sides. How many of the smaller cubes that were used to make this larger cube are now blue on one side only? How many are blue on two sides only? On three sides only?

5. Are there any smaller cubes with no blue paint in the larger cube? If so, how many?

ICE-BREAKERS

Show-Biz Bits

Arvo Ojala is the gunman Matt Dillon shoots down in the introduction of *Gunsmoke*. (Ojala is not seen in the sequence. As James Arness got older, the introduction had to be reshot twice. The Ojala introduction lasted eight years.)

Wolfman Jack's real name is Robert Smith. His start as Wolfman Jack was at Station XERP in Mexico.

The great Glenn Miller hit "PENNSYLVANIA 6-5000" was the phone number of the Pennsylvania Hotel (now Statler) in New York where Miller's band frequently appeared.

The voice of the drunk asking Judy Garland to sing "Melancholy Baby" in *A Star is Born* is Humphrey Bogart's, but an extra played the drunk.

Debbie Reynolds was Miss Burbank in 1948. Vera Miles came third in the Miss America contest that year. Zsa Zsa Gabor won Miss Hungary in 1936 but had to forgo the title because it was revealed she was not yet 16.

Oscar the Grouch's birthday (on *Sesame Street*) is June 1. Grover's is October 14, Ernie's January 28, and Bert's July 26.

The *Howdy Doody Show* first went on the air as *Puppet Playhouse*.

The Hoboken Four was the name of a quartet that had started as a trio called the Three Flashes. They became a quartet in 1935 when Frank Sinatra joined them.

The dog in RCA Victor's trademark is named Nipper. He came from Bristol, England. In 1975 the city of Baltimore sold its 5m statue of Nipper for one dollar.

Trifles and Tangents

A Novel Approach

We are all familiar with instant novels in this day of paperbacks and insta-print, but the twentieth century certainly has no corner on crest-of-the-wave publishing. When Daniel Defoe's exciting novel of 1719, *The Life and Strange Surprising Adventures of Robinson Crusoe, of York, the Mariner,* was a thunderous success, he followed in six weeks with *The Further Adventures of Robinson Crusoe.* It was, both economically and critically, a bust.

None of the following novels were, however. Try your hand.

1. Who are the missing captains?
   Captain ___________ in *The Caine Mutiny*
   Captain ___________ in *Moby Dick*, skipper of the Pequod
   Captain ___________ of the Hispaniola in *Treasure Island*
   Captain ___________ in *20,000 Leagues Under the Sea*
   Captain ___________ who terrorized Peter Pan's friends

2. Two of these three novels are based on real incidents. Which ones are they?
   Lord Jim (Conrad)
   The Bridge of San Luis Rey (Wilder)
   An American Tragedy (Dreiser)

3. Who is the author of these four titles?
   Sunday Under Three Heads
   American Notes
   The Haunted Man
   The Mystery of Edwin Drood

4. His leading protagonist was Sam Slick in a whole range of novels. Who was this novelist?

5. Who refused the Pulitzer Prize for *Arrowsmith* in 1926?

6. Match the animals listed below with their novels.
   a. He was one of the leaders of the revolt down on the farm.
   b. He sat on Long John Silver's shoulder throughout the story.

c. He was a cynical but favorite friend of Black Beauty.
d. This dog was happier in snow.
e. He almost destroyed Smiling Pond and Laughing Brook.

Ginger Paddy Major Buck Captain Flint

7. If necessity is not the mother of invention, then surely urgency is. Each of the following novels was written rather more out of need than artistic inspiration. Who were the authors?
   a. He wrote *She* in six weeks. It was a best-seller, but not in the same league as its forerunner, also set in Africa.
   b. She wrote *Eight Cousins* in just over six weeks, as much to get her family off her back (they enjoyed the revenue) as to escape the continuing need for morphine in order to sleep.
   c. *Goodbye Mr. Chips* was ignored at publication in 1934 in Britain, perhaps because it was written in four days. It did become an international smash, however.

8. Many fictional cities and towns have been made famous by novelists. Match the imaginary place in Column A, with its author in Column B

a. Deptford	Lucy Maude Montgomery
b. Crocus	Carl Barks
c. Yoknapatawpha County	Robertson Davies
d. Old Ford Duckbury	William Faulkner
e. Ingleside	W.O. Mitchell

SHERLOCK of the John

The Case of the Mystery Accident

Inspector Frank Mount peered into the distance and wondered whether he should bother to stop. After all, he was in homicide division and the mess up ahead was pretty certainly a traffic problem. Two cars, one on either shoulder, facing in opposite directions, and between them on the road, a body—a dead body—its contorted shape making clear that death had come as the result of being struck by a car. A man and a woman stood over the body, neither of them able to touch it, yet both of them drawn by the spectacle it made.

Recognizing a situation he would probably have to deal with anyway, Frank pulled over and rolled to a stop.

"Police officer!" he called getting out of his car. "Don't touch anything!"

Both the man and the woman were flushed and excited.

"I saw it happen!" the man shouted. "I saw it happen! I saw her hit him!"

"What are you saying?" the woman almost screamed.

"No, I saw her do it! I only got here a minute or two ago myself! I was coming up there from the north when I saw the old man cross the road, and she ran smack into him. I saw her!"

The woman was sobbing hard now. "He's lying. I was in there, in the field. I've been there all morning. I'm a bird-watcher. And there's a kildeer nesting by these rocks. I came to watch her. I've been here at least an hour, and I saw him hit the old man just before you came!"

"Hold it. Hold it," Frank ordered. "Just a minute. There's one way I can find out who's telling the truth. Let's start with that."

What is Frank going to do?

ICE-BREAKERS

Nothing Unbalances Better than a Belief Destroyed

The guillotine is not a French invention. Its first recorded use is in Ireland in 1307, and it was popularly used for executions in Italy and Germany long before the Reign of Terror in France.

Horace Greeley never said "Go west, young man." These words were written by John Soule in the Terre Haute, Indiana *Express* in 1851.

The Encyclopaedia Britannica was never British. It was first published in 1771 by a "Society of Gentlemen in Scotland" according to the title page. The British were involved with the eleventh edition (1910) as partners with the Americans. From 1928 to 1943, it was owned by Sears Roebuck, and from 1943 it has been the property of the University of Chicago.

Charles Darwin was not the first to theorize the idea of evolution. It was a popular idea at the time among other naturalists like Alfred Russel Wallace. Darwin, however, was first to publish.

No witches were ever burned at the stake in Salem, Mass. Twenty were executed in 1692, nineteen by hanging and one by crushing with stones.

Sir Walter Raleigh did not lay his cloak before the feet of Queen Elizabeth. (And he did not introduce tobacco to England from Virginia. In fact, he never even set foot in Virginia.)

The rickshaw is not Chinese. It was introduced into Japan in the late nineteenth century by western missionaries.

Never in any film did Tarzan say "me Tarzan—you Jane."

Walt Disney could never manage to draw Mickey Mouse properly. Mickey was first drawn by Walt's buddy Ubbe Iwerks. Walt's first choice of name for Mickey, incidentally, was Mortimer.

Nero didn't fiddle while Rome burned. Besides the fact that the fiddle wasn't invented until 1,500 years later, Nero wasn't even in Rome at the time.

IN A WORD

Rivers and Lakes, Bays and Seas

The little river of empty squares below is exactly 26 letters from source to mouth. By inserting *each* letter of the alphabet *once* into the proper square, you will have supplied the missing letter to a well-known river, lake, bay or sea (reading horizontally of course). The very first one, for example, will give you ERIE if you insert R.

Notice that in each line there are letters added just to fill up the line—and to add to the challenge.

All the bodies of water are familiar ones—except maybe the Xingu, but then how many of us paddle through Brazil?

A	W	H	N	E		I	E	T	E	C	V	O
X	T	G	Z	L	S		O	L	G	A	R	D
H	S	B	T	J	P		A	T	T	E	Q	N
O	U	Y	R	E		D	Q	G	P	A	F	K
J	E	M	X		A	L	U	J	V	B	C	H
T	L	R	C		S	P	I	A	N	V	L	U
I	E	R	P	V		I	N	G	U	T	X	G
W	L	D	J	B	S		A	N	P	E	N	Y
F	S	H	A	P	E	A		E	J	V	D	J
N	C	X	E	I	R	I	S		T	H	Y	W
B	G	T	Z	S	D	V	L		I	R	E	A
M	C	B	K	H	L	S		O	R	D	A	N
Z	K	R	D	A	N		B	E	K	C	Y	M
S	X	A	M	L		O	Z	B	Z	G	F	T
O	L	R	P		A	M	B	E	Z	I	M	Q
F	Y	E	N	Q		E	R	S	E	Y	D	I
W	H	H	G	X	T		U	I	L	L	J	O
K	G	C	Z	S	P	O		O	M	A	C	V
U	F	B	D	A	X	A	E		E	A	N	K
E	F	P	E	D	W	T	R	H		N	E	U
H	Z	L	C	P	K	X	T	I	B		R	J
R	F	W	S	T	I	G	R	I		F	I	Y
J	Y	A	M	B	B	L	A	C		R	L	G
C	V	E	W	H	U	R	O		V	O	U	B
L	B	S	Y	D	T	K		U	N	D	Y	F
S	N	W	Q	A	O	V		L	B	E	R	V

Trifles and Tangents

What's in a Name ("Nick" and Otherwise)

King Macbeth of Scotland (the real one, not Shakespeare's) had a stepson who became known as Lulach the Fatuous. Ethelred the Unready of England (968–1016) you have probably heard of. France had a Charles the Bad (1332–1387) and a Charles the Mad (1368–1422).* Even Portugal had a Ferdinand the Inconstant (1345–1383). The names that follow may not be as dramatic, but you should be able to answer most of the questions about them.

1. In the left column is the real first name. Match it with the name you know in the right column.

Lawrence	Fonzie Fonzarelli
George	Yogi Berra
John	Flip Wilson
Arthur	Kingfish Stevens
Clerow	Doc Holliday

2. What are the real names of: "The Waltz King," "The Great Imposter," "The Tennessee Plowboy," "The Iron Man," "The Legs"?

3. Ruth, Francis, Charlie O, and Worthless have something in common. Do you know what it is?

4. His real name is Mervyn A. Bogue, but he became known as Ish Kabibble. On whose radio show?

5. He was christened Andrew John Woodhouse, but he was a little devil right from the start. Whose baby was he?

6. Muhammad Ali described these boxers as "the rabbit," "the bear" and "the turtle." Who were they?

7. What is Graceland?
What is Old Betsy?
What is Little Boy?

8. Her real name was "You'll Do Lobelia," when she was born at Elm Hill Farms in Brookfield, Mass., in 1932. But she became known the world over by a different name. What name?

9. By their initials shall ye know them. Supply the full first names of
   T.S. Eliot
   B.F. Goodrich
   D.H. Lawrence
   O.J. Simpson

*Until Charles the Mad became known that way, he was called Charles the Well-Beloved.

ICE-BREAKERS

Everyone! By the Left—or the Right?

Leonardo da Vinci was left-handed. So was Jack the Ripper!

Statistically, left-handers are disproportionately represented among geniuses—and among sexual psychopaths.

Charlie McCarthy's monocle was worn on the right eye. Chester's stiff leg (in *Gunsmoke*) was the right one. Dr. Strangelove's crippled hand was the right.

Approximately 11% of the population is left-handed. But in baseball, about one-third of the pitchers are left-handed.

Babe Ruth was an outstanding left-handed pitcher for the Boston Red Sox. From 1914–19 his record was 87-44.

No left-hander has ever won the World Championship of Horseshoe Pitching since the first matches in 1909.

Sammy Davis Jr.'s glass eye is the left one. Art Carney's left ear is deaf. Captain Hook's left hand is missing. And so is Captain Ahab's left leg.

Only one of the Dionne quintuplets (Marion) was left-handed.

Neil Armstrong stepped onto the moon with his left foot first.

The vast majority of adult males put on their trousers by stepping into the left leg first.

Among the great natural advantages shared by left-handed people are writing Hebrew and unscrewing jar tops.

Special problems faced by left-handers are using scissors, playing saxophones and knitting.

Polar bears never use their right paw for attack or defense.

U.S. President James Garfield was reputed to be able to write Greek with his left hand and Latin with his right, simultaneously.

Diverting Articles

One Giant Step?

If you are old enough to read this, then you remember where you were on July 20, 1969. Probably in front of a television set watching Neil Armstrong step down onto the moon. Little children stayed up late. Professed television haters packed into their neighbors' living rooms. Travelers poured off the highways into the nearest hotel. It was an opportunity to see history; something to tell your grandchildren. One of those rare events that, for a brief time, links everyone in a common experience. Everyone except Bill Kaysing and Thomas Baron.

Baron was a pre-flight inspector with the Apollo moon landing project who insisted that the entire affair was flawed. He told a congressional investigation committee in 1967 that the Apollo mission was bothered by defective equipment and poor management. Kaysing is a writer who is convinced that the entire project was a sham, the biggest hoax ever pulled on the world. In search of proof he has pored over NASA records, interviewed scores of scientists, and appealed to the basic principles of evidence.

Why, asks Kaysing, do the photographs of the landing not show stars in the clear sky? Why did the rockets of the landing module not make a crater in the moon dust? Why is there no evidence of moon dust that Armstrong said was everywhere? Why, he goes on, is the only proof in photographs, when a naked-eye signal like a laser beam could have been relayed to Earth?

Kaysing admits there was indeed a rocketship, and it did take off from Cape Kennedy with Armstrong, Aldrin and Collins aboard, but he says the crew was jettisoned before it crashed into the south polar sea. The crew transferred to a re-entry vehicle, which was then dropped into the Pacific from a C-5A transport plane at recovery time.

Certainly the whole idea sounds insane, but don't forget this was the same government that launched the Bay of Pigs invasion and denied the presence of American troops in Vietnam. Kaysing, incidentally, has published his argument in a book called *We Never Went To the Moon*. Shortly after his testimony, Baron was found crushed to death in a car that had stalled right in the middle of a railroad crossing. There was no autopsy, and he was cremated right after.

visuthink

If

= ACACIA (a tropical tree)

and

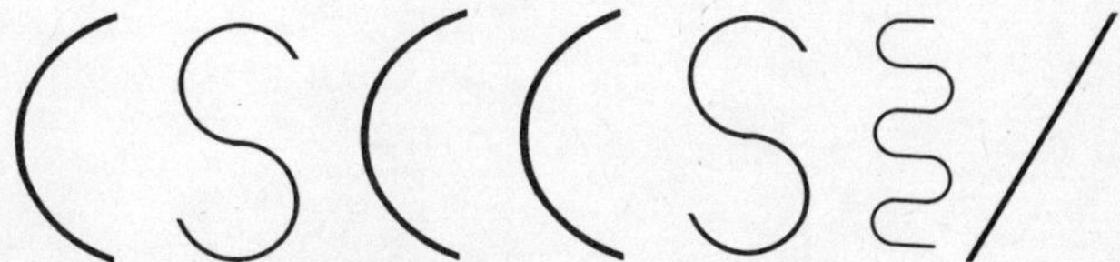

= ZYZZYVA (a tropical weevil)

What are 1?

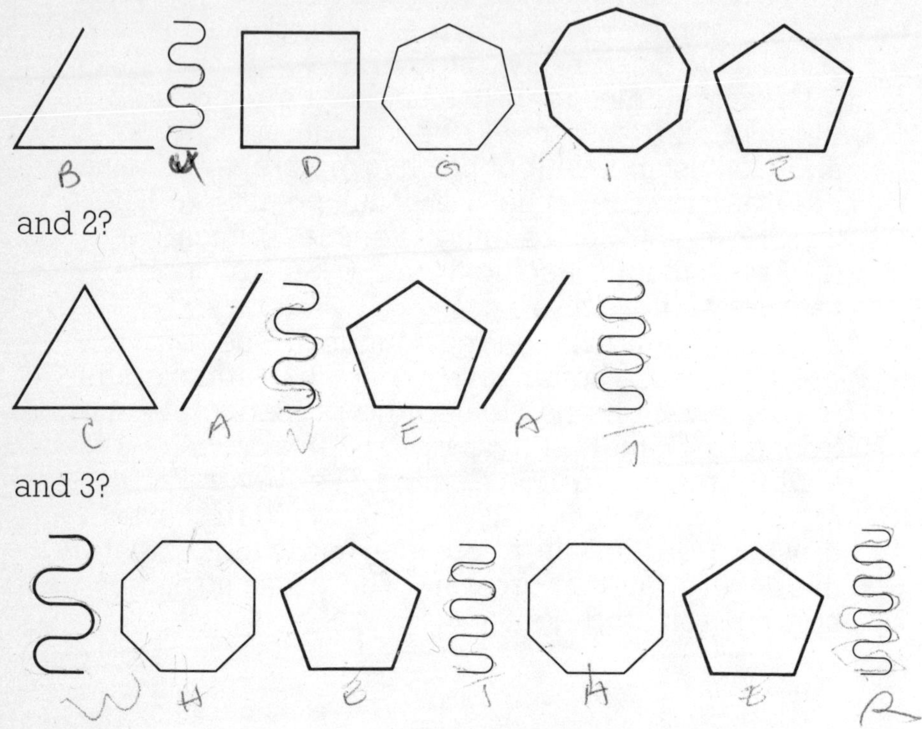

Trifles and Tangents

A Colorful Quiz

In 1958 it became the number one song throughout North America only one week after its release. Sheb Wooley wrote and sang it, and of course everyone knows his People Eater was Purple.* Now try these colors.

1. What color would you get if you mixed the Beatles' submarine with Thomas Gainsborough's famous painting of 1779?

2. This color reduces the Green Lantern to ordinary strength. (It's also the color of Dick Tracy's raincoat.)

3. It was the nightclub in San Francisco where the Kingston Trio made its first appearance (no, *not* The Hungry I)—also the Smothers Brothers, Phyllis Diller, and others.

4. This cowboy hero's little sidekick always said, "You betchum ________ ________."

5. Exactly what is the Pink Panther that got Inspector Clouseau involved in all his adventures?

6. What is the name of the Canadian pilot who shot down the Red Baron, Manfred von Richthofen, on April 21, 1918?

7. In the National and American Baseball Leagues, the National Hockey League, the National Football League, the Canadian Football League, the North American Soccer League and the National Basketball Association (keep going; this really isn't so hard!), what teams have a color in their name? Answer by league, or if you can, try the whole thing!

8. Staff Sergeant Barry Sadler wrote this, the top single of 1966.

9. This is the name of the street in London, between the Parliament Buildings and Trafalgar Square, where many government offices are located.

10. This was the biggest hit song of 1941. It has two colors in its most famous line.

11. In the War of the Roses, the Lancastrians sported a rose of one color, the Yorks, a different one. What color of rose represented each House?

12. Each of these authors wrote a book with a color in the title. We've added a clue to help (or confuse). For example, "Anna Sewell's attractive filly" would be *Black Beauty*.
   a. Chekhov's grove of trees
   b. Hawthorne's epistle
   c. Steinbeck's little horse
   d. Costain's sacred cup
   e. Kathleen Winsor's everlasting lady

*A bass voice finished the song with the guttural voicing of one word. What is that word?

Contemplator's Corner

On the outside chance that there are two of you (or three if you wish) waiting who are bored with out-dated magazines, with conversation, or even with one another, here are some simple games you can try.

Wipe-out

On a piece of paper, make 15 strokes with a pencil (or use 15 matches or toothpicks if you have them).

Take turns wiping out *one*, or *two*, or *three* strokes at a time. The object is to force your opponent to be the one who must wipe out the last stroke (or pick up the last match.)

Line-up

Draw this grid on a piece of paper. Then using 6 coins (3 for you, 3 for your opponent) place them as shown.

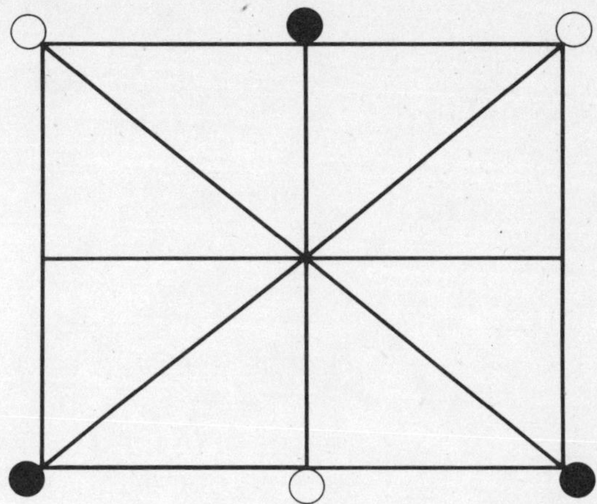

Take turns moving any *one* of your coins in any direction to any of the *next* intersections. There is no jumping. Only one coin may occupy an intersection. The object is to be first to get your coins in a straight line.

ICE-BREAKERS

Are You Sure You Want Us To Print This?

Dee-lighted! This coffee is good to the last drop!

TEDDY ROOSEVELT, 1907
(YES. AFTER A CUP OF MAXWELL HOUSE!)

One of the finest and most poetical views I have ever seen.

ARNOLD BENNETT,
ENGLISH NOVELIST, 1912
(HE WAS LOOKING DOWN AT TOLEDO, OHIO.)

The only job in the whole world I want to do is acting. Offer me ten times the money for doing something else and I'd refuse. I'd lack self-confidence because I'd be in the wrong job.

RONALD REAGAN, 1942

Americans require a restful quiet in the moving-picture theater and . . . talking on the screen destroys the illusion . . . the idea is not practical.

THOMAS EDISON, 1926

They couldn't hit an elephant at this dist_________.

MAJOR-GENERAL JOHN SEDGWICK AT BATTLE OF SPOTSYLVANIA, 1864

I wish the bald eagle had not been chosen (as a symbol of the U.S.); he is a bird of bad moral character; he does not get his living honestly.

BENJAMIN FRANKLIN, 1782 (FRANKLIN ARGUED FOR THE TURKEY, WHICH HE SAID WAS MORE AMERICAN IN SPIRIT.)

It is the duty of politicians to climb the tree and shake down the acorns to the pigs below.

SIR JOHN A. MACDONALD, 1876

The Duke of Wellington had a strong objection to railroads. One of his stated reasons: "They encourage the lower classes to move about."

In point of intellect the average woman cannot reason and think. But she can argue.

STEPEHN LEACOCK, 1926

The great question that has never been answered, and which I have not been able to answer despite my 30 years of research into the feminine soul is: What does a woman want?

SIGMUND FREUD, 1932

Come on, boys! We've got the damn Yankees on the run!

GEN. JOSEPH WHEELER, USM (WHILE LEADING A CHARGE AGAINST THE SPANISH AT LAS GUASIMAS, CUBA, ON JUNE 24, 1898.)

Let Arabs and Jews settle their differences like good Christians.

U.S. AMBASSADOR WARREN AUSTIN, 1948

SHERLOCK of the John

The Case on Pioneer Farm

"Have I missed much?" Doug Doyle asked as he slid into the bench marked "For Representatives of The Press and Media." "My car wouldn't start again, and by the time I got a cab, the court must have been in session already. Then to top it off the cabbie was a complete greenhorn. He didn't even know where the county courthouse is! It's going to be one of those days."

Trevor Hawkes leaned a little closer as the buzz in the courtroom grew gradually louder. He and Doyle had been reporters on rival newspapers for a long time now and were generous about sharing information.

"Well, you've missed a bit. Chadwell declared this recess about five minutes ago, and there was only one witness and that was Brunt himself. He's already given his story. Good too! One heck of a witness on his own behalf."

"Great," Doyle said, "just what I needed. Missed the whole testimony."

"Yes, but what Brunt said today is really no different from what we reported when the thing happened," Hawkes replied. "I told you he was a good witness for himself. Judge Chadwell even said so."

Doyle looked up. "*You* reported the original. I was on vacation. My first August break in years."

"Oh that's right." Hawkes nodded. "To be honest I wasn't at the farm myself when it happened. One of our new kids did the legwork."

"As I remember it," Doyle said, "Brunt was the off-hours security guard at Pioneer Farm, and he killed the manager down at the barn one evening around sunset. Hit him with a big stick didn't he?"

"Yes, he admits all that. But he's arguing accident," Hawkes said, "and there's a lot on his side. First of all, there had been a lot of break-ins and vandalism at the Farm, particularly around the log barn where the animals are. Some of that antique pioneer stuff is very valuable too. You remember, one guard was beaten up a few months ago. Brunt says he was jumpy, and he had reason to be too."

Doyle continued. "The place doesn't open to the public until 10 a.m., as I remember, and only the manager and his wife live on the site. Wasn't there something about the wife in this case?"

"Only that she's more Brunt's age than her husband's," Hawkes replied, "and that's raised a few eyebrows. You should see her! Anyway, Brunt says he always made a circuit of the building at sunset, after the place closes, and on this night he saw an old threshing flail on the manure pile. He figures some kid dragged it out of the barn. Then just as he picked it up there was somebody standing over him. With the setting sun in his eyes, he couldn't see who it was, so he just swung with the flail to protect himself. Of course it was the manager, and that was that. What a way to end! Right on a manure pile!"

"Not a bad story at all," Doyle said. "Only one hole in it that I can see. I wonder how much of a farmer Judge Chadwell is? You know, maybe today may not be such a disaster after all."

What is the hole in Brunt's story that Doug Doyle has noticed?

Trifles and Tangents

Let the Battle Rage

Among the military leaders celebrated in legend and song is the "very model of a modern major-general" that Gilbert and Sullivan gave us in the *Pirates of Penzance* (1879). G & S maintained they were being very specific in that song. Their subject was Viscount Garnet Wolseley, an important British officer who fought at Sebastapol, in the Sepoy Mutiny, at Khartoum, Natal and Cyprus, among other places. In 1870, Wolseley led the expedition across Upper Canada to quell the Red River Rebellion of Louis Riel and his Métis people.

Whether or not Wolseley was conversant with "matters animal, vegetable and mineral" pales beside his resourcefulness. No one in the expedition knew exactly how to find the Red River settlement, so Wolseley hired Métis to lead the way!

Now try these military riddles.

1. Match the location with the battle and date. In each case, the first mentioned is the attacker.

a. Henry V of England defeats the French, 1415	Austerlitz
b. Russians and Austrians lose to the French, 1805	Marathon
c. The Holy League defeats the Turks, 1571	Philippi
d. British lose badly to Zulu nation, 1879	Tannenburg
e. Persian forces lose to Athenians, 490 BC.	Lepanto
f. Russian 2nd army eliminated by Germany, 1914	Isandhlwana
g. Mark Antony and Octavius defeat Brutus and Cassius, 42 BC.	Agincourt

2. *a.* At what battle did Lord Nelson signal "England expects every man to do his duty"?

b. After this famous incident during the battle at Balaclava, Tennyson wrote: "Theirs not to reason why, Theirs but to do and die."

c. During the battle of the USS *Chesapeake* and the HMS *Shannon*, American captain James Lawrence uttered the famous cry: "Don't give up the ship!" During what war was this?

d. As the Battle of Waterloo was falling to the Anglo-Dutch and Prussian forces, Wellington called for the surrender of Napoleon's famous and most trusted Imperial Guard. What was the reply of their commander, General Cambronne?

3. *a.* In 1968 this North Vietnamese general demonstrated his shrewd perception of the American psyche in an offensive (the Tet) that gained almost no territory, cost some 60,000 soldiers, and failed to stir up the intended general uprising. Yet it showed the United States it would never win the war. This general's name?

b. The Somme, 1916, is still held as the bloodiest battle ever. From July 1 to November 19, it cost over a million men and accomplished nothing. Who were the British and French commanders of this pointless slaughter?

c. When General James Wolfe died at the Battle of the Plains of Abraham in 1759, he was not, as is often thought, the commander-in-chief of His Majesty's forces in North America. Who was?

d. This incredibly able general only lost one battle in his very busy career: Châlons in AD 451 (unless you count the fact that he died of a heart attack during intercourse on his wedding night).

visuthink

First, check your watch. If it's too early in the morning, or too late at night, don't even try this one. But if you aren't too tired, it's a very rewarding problem and a real test of your patience.

1. How many triangles are there in the figure below?

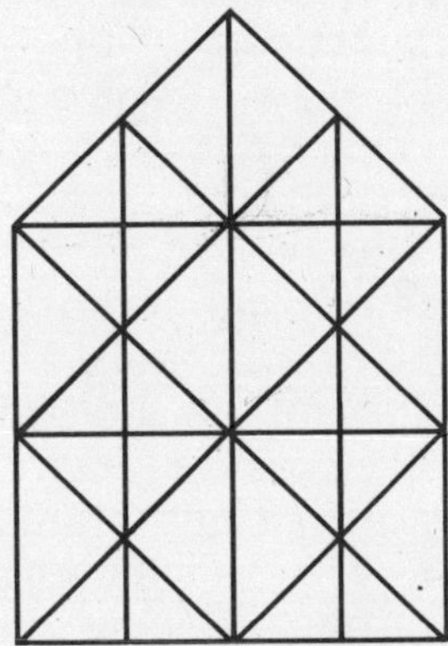

2. Don't even bother trying to count the triangles in this one. (But if you *really* want to, we do give the answer.) What we are interested in is to see if you can tell, *without* using a ruler or pencil or even your finger, how many straight lines it took to produce this figure.

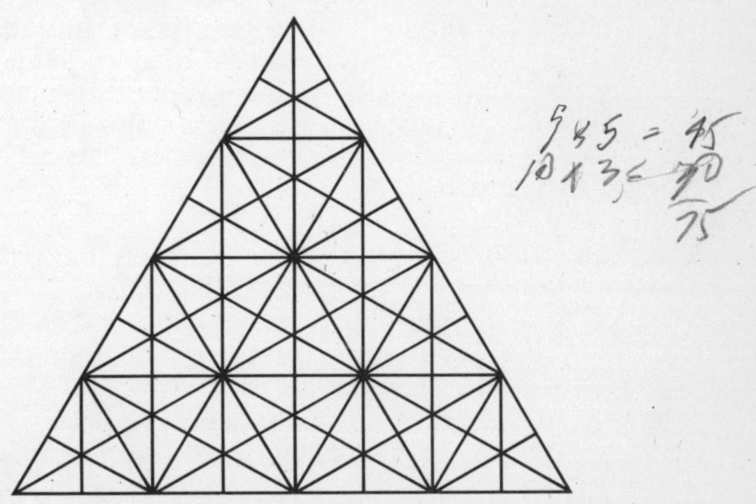

Diverting Articles

It Isn't Over until It's Over

Among the other nineteenth-century millionaires you probably have never heard of—and why should you—belongs the name of George Bateson. His was a household name in Victorian England, however, for it was this man who in 1852 patented the Bateson Life Revival Device: "A device of proven efficacy, in countless instances in this country and abroad." "Bateson's belfry," as it came to be known, was nothing more than an iron bell with a wire cord attached. The bell was for mounting on the top of a coffin; the cord fed through the lid and was tied to the dead person's hand. It provided an unmistakable means of communication on the outside chance that the dead person really was not dead.

Lest there be even a hint that Bateson belongs on humankind's endless list of forgotten entrepreneurs, you should know that Queen Victoria granted him an OBE for his work in 1859. That was how deeply he was appreciated, because for the people of the nineteenth century, fear of premature burial had become an absolute obsession. It was not just because of the work of Edgar Allen Poe, although no doubt his macabre material fueled their concerns. Rather, the terror of being buried alive grew from real and not uncommon evidence.

A reasonably typical case in point was that of a ten-year-old boy in Wales who presumably had drowned. At his funeral, the press reported:

> while the coffin lay in the open grave, and the first earth was shovelled upon it, a most frightful noise and kicking ensued from within. The sextons ceased their labours and caused the coffin to be opened, whereupon the lad stepped out and called for his parents.

That was in 1853. And the boy in question had indeed been declared dead by a doctor who insisted that there had been no respiration or pulse, and that the skin was cold and gray. No wonder the Victorians had more trust in Bateson's ingenuity than in medical science.

Indeed, it was an era of fairly primitive understanding for doctors. They knew disturbingly little about stroke, or epilepsy, or narcolepsy. Not until the middle of the twentieth century was it fully understood that cardiac arrest can be wholly reversible.

Thus the Victorians dealt with their anxiety in two ways. The first, least attractive but most certain, was simply to wait until the evidence of death was unmistakable. But confirmation by odor was unsatisfactory for any number of reasons, so the Victorians turned to technology. Spring-loaded caskets were popular for the wealthy who were buried above ground in vaults. A system of wires ensured that the slightest movement of the body would throw open the coffin lid. Naturally, post mortem spasm, a common occurrence the Victorians also did not understand, threw open a lot of coffins and only heightened the uncertainty about premature burial.

Other techniques open to the wealthy included posting a servant at the grave, on night and day watch for a month or more. This method, made functional by running a length of iron pipe from the coffin to the ground above, would ensure a response if the deceased should suddenly come to and need help. The poor, obviously unable to adopt such techniques, often employed a simpler tactic. They would bury their relatives with a shovel or iron bar on the uncertain premise that since there would be no servant on standby to help, they could dig themselves out of their confining state.

Bateson's device, then, was a welcome one. It was simple, inexpensive and efficient—at least theoretically. The "belfry" became a top seller. All of which leads to the inevitable question: Did Bateson put one on his own coffin?

As it turned out, no one was more terrified of being buried alive than Bateson himself, and his workshop turned out increasingly elaborate prototypes for installation on his own coffin. By 1867 he was quite mad. After writing directions in his will that he be cremated, he developed a suspicion that his instructions would be ignored. In the spring of 1868 he soaked himself with linseed oil, set himself aflame, and died by self-immolation.

More Fame(ous) Wit

William Tell wore contacts

Euclid was square

Socrates is an orange pekoe freak

Snoopy has fleas

Pension off Peter Pan

Leda hates her duvet

Adam was Eve's mother (And you think you've got problems?)

Marshall McLuhan is linear and strictly sequential

Jean Piaget developed erratically

Cinderella married for money

Isaac Newton counts on his fingers

Lassie kills chickens

Copernicus is off-center

Hey Atreus! It's time for lunch!

Maria Montessori tot me to rite wen I wuz only too

Wrong-way Corrigan is in charge of the baggage

Pythagoras' idea is strictly based on hype

How to One-up a TPA*

This is a very special section, designed specifically for a very special kind of person: the TPA or *trivia pain-in-the-ass*. Trivia *freaks* are OK, because they enjoy trivia for its own sake. Even trivia fanatics are fun because they will listen to *your* trivia. But a TPA is that person who *always* knows the trivia piece that you have—or at least pretends to—and then *always* comes back with another piece that you couldn't possibly know. A TPA waits for this opportunity and pounces on it—and you—with glee.

Here's your revenge. All the questions that follow are designed to sucker-punch TPAs because they are ones that TPAs are certain to know, or at least they'll pretend to. Then when they're hooked (this type wouldn't dare admit ignorance) you deliver the knockout: a related piece of trivia they'll never get! For example, you shyly ask who it was that went down with Buddy Holly and Ritchie Valens in rock 'n roll's worst-ever plane crash. (You might even add that it was on February 3, 1959.) Now for sure, TPAs will know it was the Big Bopper, and almost for sure, they'll try to one-up you with the fact that the Big Bopper's real name was J.P. Richardson. Maybe even with the fact that the J. stood for "Jape."

Even if they don't come back with a one-upper, you've still sucker-punched them. So deliver the knockout. Ask, "Who gave up his seat on that twin-engine Beech Bonanza so that the Big Bopper could get to Fargo, North Dakota, for a concert?"

(It was Waylon Jennings, then of The Crickets.)

See how easy it is! One or two of these and they'll be cured. But just to be sure, we have given you enough to cover all situations and all types of TPAs.

1. *The Sucker Punch:* What was the O'Hara's family plantation called in *Gone With the Wind*
(It was Tara. This is a dead giveaway for a TPA.)

   The Knock-Out: OK. Then what was the name of the plantation where Ashley Wilkes' family lived?
(It was Twelve Oaks. And if you need it, Margaret Mitchell's working name for Tara was Fontenoy Hall. It didn't become Tara until just before publication.)

---

*Trivia Pain-in-the Ass

2. *The SP:* The seventh Earl of Cardigan became famous for what military incident involving the Russians?
(He led the Charge of the Light Brigade.)

The KO: And what was the real name of the Light Brigade?
(The 11th Light Dragoons. If you really want to smear the TPA ask him how many men were in the charge. He'll know that Tennyson said "Into the valley of death rode the SIX HUNDRED." But there were 673! 113 were killed and 134 wounded.)

3. *The SP:* While we're on Tennyson and the Light Brigade—and since you did so badly—how did Tennyson start his famous poem?
("Half a league, half a league, half a league onward")

The KO: How long is a league?
(Three miles. And a chain is 66 feet, and a furlong is 660 feet, but don't use that if the TPA is already on the ropes.)

4. *The SP:* What is the name of Liberace's brother?
(George. The TPA will probably try to put you on ice by adding that Liberace's birth name is Wladziu Valentino, or at least he'll note that Liberace's parents were Italian and Polish. If he does, go for the KO.)

The KO: What's Liberace's legal name?
(No. Not Lee Liberace. The Lee is only a nickname. His legal name is just Liberace.)

5. *The SP:* What famous team began in Chicago in 1927 with players like "Toots" Wright, "Fats" Long, "Kid" Oliver, and "Runt" Pullens?
(The Harlem Globetrotters, founded by Abe Saperstein.)

The KO: When "Bunny" Levitt and Bob Karstens played for the Globetrotters, what was so special about them?
(Along with Abe Saperstein they were the only whites who ever played on the team.)

6. *The SP:* Prime ministers of Canada and presidents of the United States are usually stuck with the name that history or the media gives them. King, for example, is never known as William King or Harrison as William Harrison. How are they known?
(As William Lyon Mackenzie King or just Mackenzie King, and as William Henry Harrison.)

The KO: Then how about the B and the G in Rutherford B. Hayes and Warren G. Harding or the R.B. and the B in R.B. Bennett and Lester B. Pearson?
(Rutherford Birchard Hayes and Warren Gamaliel Harding. Richard Bedford Bennett and Lester Bowles Pearson. Bowles, incidentally, is pretty easy. If you need it, there's always John David Sparrow Thompson, prime minister from 1892–94.)

7. *The SP:* Who played Commander Nelson on the *Seaview* in the top-rated *Voyage To The Bottom of the Sea* series?
(Richard Basehart.)

The KO: The series was set in the future. What year?
(1983. If you need it, one of the supporting cast of the series gradually worked his role into semi-star billing by playing a slow-witted but reliable able seaman. His name on the show? Kowalski.)

8. *The SP:*
   a. 1937 was a busy year. Another of the Great Powers withdrew from the League of Nations. Which one?
   (Italy.)
   b. The Spanish town of Guernica was immortalized in 1937, first by the Nazis and then by whom?
   (Picasso).
   c. Walt Disney produced a famous full-length cartoon that year.
   (*Snow White and the Seven Dwarfs.*)
   d. Steinbeck turned to Robert Burns' poetry for a title to his novel of that year. What novel?
   (*Of Mice and Men.*)

The KO: (Don't be concerned. A full-fledged TPA will get all of those above. He'll really be on a roll now, so . . .) What did George Biro do in 1937?
(He introduced his invention, the ballpoint pen.)

9. *The SP:* There's a fairly standard way to distinguish alligators from crocodiles. What is it?
(The snout. Alligators' are shorter and broader. Crocodiles' are longer and narrow.)

The KO: What is special about both alligators and crocodiles in the reptile world?
(They are the only reptiles with a voice-making capacity. They bellow. All others merely hiss.)

10. *The SP:* Of course you know that Josef Stalin's real name was not Stalin.
(It was Dzhugashvili.) Now, if your subject even tries to spell this because he knows the answer, let him off the hook; he's a trivia freak not a TPA. If he can pronounce it, proclaim him a national treasure. But if he bluffs, give him another certain SP.

Stalin was not Russian either, was he?
(He was Georgian. A trivia freak won't have to bluff this.)

The KO: When Stalin was expelled from school in 1899, where was he studying?
Tiflis Theological Seminary. Official Party word was that he was tossed out for reading Marxist pamphlets. His mother said he had to leave because of ill health. You probably won't need this, but just in case: Stalin regarded his oldest son Yakov as a patsy and even rejected Wermacht offers to repatriate him after his capture in World War II. Yakov died in a German POW camp.)

11. *The SP:* On November 1, 1959, he became the first NHL goalie to wear a face mask regularly in all games. He put it on after Andy Bathgate smashed his face with a slapshot eight minutes into the game. Who was that goalie?
(Jacques Plante of the Montreal Canadiens.)

The KO: Canadiens' coach "Toe" Blake had forbidden Plante to wear the mask in games up to this point. What did Plante do in his debut with the Canadiens in 1952 that Coach Dick Irwin soon forbade?
(He wore a toque. In a scramble around the net, the toque would come off and Plante was known to have gone for the hat instead of the puck.)
Just for the record, the very first goalie to wear a face mask in a game was Clint Benedict of the Montreal Maroons in 1929. And you won't need this—but what the heck, a sports TPA is the worst kind—Stan Mikita and Bobby Hull were NOT the first to use curved sticks. That honor belongs to Harry Cameron of the Toronto St. Patricks in the 1920s.

12. *The SP:* Who wrote "T'was the Night Before Christmas"? (Clement C. Moore in 1822. This is standard fare for a TPA.)

The KO: But Moore was not a poet. What was his profession?
(He was Professor of Oriental and Greek Literature at General Theological Seminary in New York. The original title of the poem was "A Visit From St. Nicholas," and it was published without Moore's knowledge in the Troy *Sentinel* on December 23, 1823.)

Rabbit Punches or Flinging at Fatuosity

13. A full-blown TPA thrives on debunking popular beliefs and sayings and facts that are wrong, even though they have been thoroughly worked into our culture. Things like: Delilah did not cut off Samson's hair (see Judges, 16:19). Also, she didn't seduce him as much as nag him. And things like: Sherlock Holmes never once said, "Elementary, my dear Watson"; the Magna Carta was not signed at the bottom (it was sealed); Richard III was not a hunchback.

You should be able to turn the tables with these quickies.

a. Who introduced the assembly-line manufacturing technique to the automobile industry?
(Standard answer is Henry Ford. It was Ransom E. Olds in 1901.)

b. Who were Adam and Eve's children?
(Cain and Abel. And Seth. Adam (there is no mention of Eve in this one) is also credited with a number of sons and daughters in Genesis 5.)

c. Whose line in *Henry IV, Part I* is "Discretion is the better part of valour"?
(Falstaff. But what he *said* was, "The better part of valour is discretion" (V, iv, 120).)

d. Where was the "Desiderata" (Go placidly amid the noise and haste) found?
(In Old St. Paul's Church, Baltimore in 1692. Or so 'tis said. Actually it was written and copyrighted by Max Ehrmann in 1927.)

e. Who made the first non-stop flight across the Atlantic?
(Not Lindbergh. He was, in fact, the 67th! Alcock and Brown flew first from St. John's, Newfoundland, to Ireland in 1919. In the same year thirty-four crossed in a British dirigible, and in 1924, thirty-three in a German dirigible. Lindbergh's in 1927 was the first *solo* flight.)

f. How did "Black" Jack Pershing get his name?
(Not from his disposition, sour as it was, but from his years of service with the Tenth Cavalry, a black regiment. His original name, thankfully forgotten, was Nigger Jack.)

g. What was the first day of the sixteenth century?
(Not January 1, 1500, but January 1, 1501. From January 1, year 1 to December 31, year 99, was only 99 years. Figure it out.)

14. *The SP:* What famous storytellers have given us *Little Red Riding Hood*?
(Yes, the Brothers Grimm. It was Rotkäppchen #26, but. . .)

The KO: Where did *they* get it?
(The earliest version of the story came from Charles Perrault in 1697, the man who gave classic form to Cinderella, Sleeping Beauty, and others. In Perrault's version the story ends when the wolf eats Red Riding Hood.)

15. *The SP:* Who made this famous comment about General Ambrose Burnside: "Only Burnside could have managed such a coup, wringing one last spectacular defeat from the jaws of victory"?
(Abraham Lincoln after the Battle of the Crater, July 30, 1864.)

The KO: Just how did Burnside manage to turn a victory into a defeat?
(He tunneled under the dug-in Confederate troops, set off a huge pile of explosives, which made an enormous hole in the ground, and left the Southerners totally befuddled and ripe for defeat. Then Burnside ordered his troops *into* the crater where they could barely maneuver and couldn't escape. The Confederates then called up reinforcements to the edge of the crater and began picking off their enemies at will. The final figure was a horrendous 4,000 Yankee dead.)

16. *The SP:* Along with Daisy and her pups, Blondie and Dagwood had two children. What were their names?
(Alexander and Cookie.)

The KO: Alexander was born on the April 15, 1934 show, but he had a different name for the next year or so. What was that name?
(He was called Baby Dumpling. Cookie, incidentally was born in 1941. Dagwood's boss was J.C. Dithers. If you need it, J.C. stood for Julius Caesar.)

17. *The SP:* What heavyweight boxing match in Lewiston, Maine, ended with a famous mystery punch at 1 minute, 57 seconds of the first round?
(Cassius Clay over Sonny Liston in 1965. Many of the ringside patrons had not yet found their seats!)

The KO: Lewiston, Maine, was also the site of the shortest ever professional boxing match. Do you know what happened?
(On September 29, 1946, Ralph Walton was still slipping in his mouthpiece when the bell rang. His opponent, Al Couture, dashed across the ring and decked him with one devastating punch. Including the count, the fight lasted ten and one half seconds.)

18. *The SP:* There are two one-eyed jacks in a deck of playing cards. Which suits?
(The jack of spades and jack of hearts are one-eyed.)

The KO: How many jacks' eyes are visible altogether in a deck of playing cards?
(Twelve.)

19. *The SP: Star Trek* freaks are in a class all their own. They'll all know, for example, that Warp Factor One is the speed of light, and that Warp Factor Eight is 512 times the speed of light. Ask, What is the maximum safe cruising speed of the *Enterprise*?
(Warp Factor Six. 218 times the speed of light. A good Trivia freak will answer and leave it there. A TPA will try to one up that, so use the KO.)

The KO: In what year was warp speed first used?
(2018.)

20. *The SP:* Mattel Inc. had such success with Barbie (the doll) that they brought out her friends soon after. How many can you name?
(Ken, Kelly, Skipper, Francie and P.J.)

The KO: Only one of them had a last name. Which one?
(Ken Thurston.)

21. *The SP:* It's only happened once in major league ball. Three brothers took to the outfield for the San Francisco Giants on September 22, 1963. Who?
(Matty, Felipe and Jesus Alou.)

The KO: You have a choice here. One is a gentle KO; the second is a good body punch. There has been only one other three-brother combination in the big leagues. Who?
(Joe, Vince, and Dom Dimaggio.)
What is the Alou brothers' real last name?
(Rojas.)

22. *The SP:* Humphrey Bogart and Katharine Hepburn went down the Ulanga River in a 1951 movie. What movie?
(*The African Queen*.)

The KO: According to standard navigational practice, was the left bank of the Ulanga on their left or on their right in the movie?
(Going *down* a river (i.e. with the current) the left bank is on the left. If you want to, toss in that the Ulanga empties into the Bora River. Bogart's name in the movie, by the way, was Charlie Allnut, and Hepburn's was Rose Sayer.)

23. *The SP:* It is well known that of the five countries to suffer the most battle deaths in World War II, Germany is not first, but second. What country is first?
(The Soviet Union, at over six million battle deaths, almost doubles Germany's figure of 3¼ million.)

The KO: How many of the other three countries can you name?
(China is third, at 1⅓ million, followed by Japan, 1¼ million, and Poland, 664,000. Britain is sixth, and the United States ninth, after Romania and Yugoslavia. According to the *World Book of Odds*, Romania's was the worst army to be in. Odds against being killed were 1 to 1. (By comparison, odds for a Japanese soldier were 7 to 1.)

24. *The SP:* Hockey, more than any other sport, seems to invite nicknames. At least it did in the heyday of the NHL before the modern day gong show replaced it. For example, you remember *Walter* Broda and *Harvey* Jackson, or *Fred* Taylor and *Lorne* Worsley. They were never called by

their first names. What were they called?
(Turk Broda, Busher Jackson, Cyclone Taylor, Gump Worsley.)

The KO: The New York Rangers' goalie for most of the 1942 season was Steve Buzinski. His nickname?
(He was dubbed "The-Puck-Goes-Inski." Buzinski was noticeably bowlegged and short for a goalie, but because of World War II, the Rangers had no other candidates, despite his 6.11 goals against average.)

25. *The SP:* Humphrey Bogart never did say "Play it again, Sam" in *Casablanca*. What did he say?
(After Ingrid Bergman asked Sam to play "As Time Goes By" (she said "Play it, Sam"), Bogart said, "You played it for her; you can play it for me . . . play it!" This is a piece of cake for a TPA. So is the fact that Gary Cooper did NOT say "Smile when you say that" in *The Virginian*, but "If you want to call me that, smile." You need the KO.

The KO: What famous general reputedly explained his success with the statement, "Git thar fustest with the mostest!"?
(Your TPA will say Nathan Bedford Forrest, Confederate general, whereupon you patiently explain that Forrest was a very literate, well-spoken gentleman, and because he was self-educated, would have been mortified at such sub-standard speech. Forrest would never have expressed himself that way.)

26. *The SP:* Ann Landers and Dear Abby (Abigail Van Buren) not only share top billing as consultants of the heart, they share something else. What?
(Parents. They are sisters.)

The KO: What were they christened by their parents?
(Ann was christened Esther Pauline and Abby was christened Pauline Esther.)

27. *The SP:* What is the magic word that changes Billy Batson into Captain Marvel and back again?
(SHAZAM!)

The KO: What do the letters of "SHAZAM!" stand for?
(*S*olomon-wisdom, *H*ercules-strength, *A*tlas-stamina, *Z*eus-

power, *A*chilles-courage, *M*ercury-speed. If your subject is a trivia freak rather than a TPA, you can entertain him with the additional fact that Captain Marvel's name was changed to SHAZAM after a suit launched by National comics who claimed he looked too much like Superman.)

28. *The SP:* Perhaps the greatest ruler in African history, he crushed the Italian army at Adwa (or Aduwa) in 1896, and established modern Ethiopia. Who?
(Emperor Menelik II.)

The KO: Menelik had a somewhat extreme eccentricity. Do you know what it was?
(When he was ill, he would eat a few pages of the Bible to restore his strength. After a stroke in December 1913, he ate the entire Book of Kings (an Egyptian publication). His death immediately after was complicated by a bowel obstruction.)

29. *The SP:* Until Genuine Risk won the Kentucky Derby in 1980, the only filly ever to do it before was *who* in 1915?
(Regret, in the unspectacular time of 2:05.2.)

The KO: What movie star made Regret even more famous by claiming a relationship with her?
(Francis the Talking Mule said she was his mother, especially in the 1951 movie *Francis Goes to the Races*.)

30. For this one, make up your own SP.
It isn't hard to find at least one trivial fact about Karl Marx, David Livingstone, Elizabeth Taylor and Alfred the Great, but what is the one thing they had in common?
(They all suffered from hemorrhoids. Elizabeth Taylor had surgery twice. David Livingstone refused surgery for fear he would be disabled and thus kept from returning to Africa. Livingstone is reputed to have died from the affliction. Karl Marx once wrote to Engels, during the composing of *Das Kapital*: "To finish I must at least be able to sit down." King Alfred once prayed for a disease that would suppress his lust but not his capacity as a ruler. The chronicles of the day also report he prayed later for relief.)

Rib-Kickers

There is a class of TPAs that won't leave you alone—even when you've had enough. The few quickies here are to shut them up if necessary—or, if you are feeling vengeful, for your use when you have them down after a KO.

1. Who is the most famous alumnus of Disco Tech?
(Batman. Worth noting is that on the old Bullwinkle Show, Rocky the Squirrel and Bullwinkle Moose were often involved in college football games: Wossamatta U. vs Disco Tech. But there is no evidence that either ever graduated. Your question asked for an *alumnus*.)

2. On June 23, 1917, Ernie Shore of the Boston Red Sox went into the record books. Why?
(The only relief pitcher ever to throw a perfect game. Babe Ruth was the starter and threw four balls to the leadoff hitter. Ruth argued with umpire Brick Owens, then punched him, and was tossed out. Shore came in to throw perfect ball to 27 batters.)

3. When does "time immemorial" start, legally?
(In AD 1189, the first year of Richard I's reign, and then goes back in time from there. This became English law in a statute of AD 1275.)

4. What country sits on the largest subterranean water reservoir in the world?
(Egypt. The fact was confirmed by geologists in 1976, but the water is too hard to get at.)

5. Each one of the following became special in history for some reason. Do you know why?
   a. Warwick Kerr in 1956?
   (He was crossbreeding 70 lethal African bees with native bees in Sao Paulo, Brazil. Twenty-six escaped to start the phenomenon that has become known as "Killer Bees.")
   b. Larry Doby in 1947?
   (He was the *second* black player in major league baseball after Jackie Robinson. Doby made the all-star team six years in a row.)

c. Mary Anne Nichols in 1888?
(She became the first victim of Jack the Ripper in London, on August 31. Her nickname was "Polly.")

d. Ray Goodwin in 1972?
(He won the "most unusual entry" prize of the British Wildlife Recording Society for two years in a row, thus being the only entrant ever to do so. His best tape was of a Roman snail eating a lettuce leaf.)

e. Charles Darrow in 1933?
(He presented his idea for a game called "Monopoly" to Parker Bros.)

6. Jean Paul Sartre and Simone de Beauvoir starred in a stage play called *Desire Caught By The Tail* in 1941. It was one of the greatest duds of all time. Who wrote it?
(Pablo Picasso.)

7. What was the real name of French vaudeville star "Le Petomane"?
(Joseph Pujol, 1851–1945, who headlined at the Moulin Rouge from 1892–1914 because of his well-tempered derriere. Pujol could—well—*fart* with amazing talent. For part of his act he gave flatulent impressions of contemporary opera stars, played an ocarina through a rubber tube, and could blow out a candle with one of his zephyrs at a distance of one foot. For an encore, which was always demanded, he would ask his audience to remain standing, while he solemnly farted the first line of the "Marseillaise." Lest you think Pujol was just a puff of curiosity, he was able to outdraw Sarah Bernhardt 3 to 1 in audience size.)

Go Ahead: Everyone Will Believe You!

From 1931 to the beginning of war in the Pacific, the final examination of the Japanese Naval Academy presented the following question: "How would you carry out a surprise attack on Pearl Harbor?"

Aristotle (384–322 BC), who is widely acknowledged as one of the founders of western scientific thought, once said that women's mouths have fewer teeth than men's. The idea was accepted for centuries and was even part of the curriculum in medieval universities.

At the Brussels World Fair in 1958, a comparison study was made between a North American car and the Russian *Ziss*. A neutral engineer judged the American car to be superior, with the Russian car a fairly distant second. The official Soviet news agency *Tass* reported it thus for the folks back home: "In comparison tests of Russian and foreign automobiles, the Ziss placed second while the American car was next to last."

Mount Everest, when first measured from the southern view, showed to be exactly 29,000 feet high, but surveyors, fearful that they would be accused of imprecision, are said to have falsely reported the height as 29,020 feet.

Pythagoras (c.582–c.507 BC) once argued that earthquakes were caused by dead people fighting in the underworld.

Alexander Graham Bell was just as interested in flying as he was in communication. But he was committed to the idea that the answer to powered flight for humankind lay in kites: Long after his own company successfully flew a motor-powered airplane, Bell continued to develop kites, some of them so large they had to be launched by teams of galloping horses.

Pliny the Elder (AD 23–79) whose 37-volume encyclopedia of natural science was a dominant force for centuries, wrote that bears were born as tiny bits of claws and unformed flesh, and were licked into shape by their mothers. Pliny was one of the first Roman scientists to argue for observation as a technique for studying natural phenomena.

Trifles and Tangents

Odd One Out

Royal names by and large are dull. And certainly repetitive. The famous Cleopatra, for example, was actually Cleopatra VII of the Macedonian dynasty. She married her younger brother Ptolemy XIII (don't be harsh; it was expected of her), and four years later, an even younger brother, Ptolemy XIV. Of her four children—one by Julius Caesar, three by Mark Antony—there was a boy named Ptolemy and a girl—you guessed it—named Cleopatra. But then the ancient Egyptians were hard to understand. The rulers below should be easier for you.

Each list contains one name that does not belong. In the first list, for example, Stephen may not belong (or is it William IV?) as a ruler of England.

Rulers of England
Edward IV
Stephen
William IV
James III
Richard III

Emperors of Rome
Marcus Aurelius
Philip the Arab
Diocletian
Domitian
Publius Vergilius Maro

Presidents of the United States
James Buchanan
Rutherford Hayes
Chester Arthur
Asher Benjamin
Franklin Pierce

Prime Ministers of Canada
John Sparrow Thompson
Charles Tupper
Charles Gladstone
John Joseph Abbott
Mackenzie Bowell

Premiers of the USSR
Georgi Malenkov
Nikolai Bulganin
Leon Trotsky
Aleksei Kosygin
Nikita Kruschev

Secretaries-General of the United Nations
Lester Pearson
Dag Hammarskjöld
U Thant
Kurt Waldheim
Trygve Lie

English Monarchies
House of Plantagenet
House of Lancaster
House of Hanover
House of Saxony
House of York

Rulers of France
Louis XVIII
Philip VII
Henry IV
Charles X
Napoleon III

Triple Crown Winners
Northern Dancer
Seattle Slew
Sir Barton
Assault
Citation

The Irreverent Graffiti Page

God is dead!
—Nietzsche
Nietzsche is dead. Ha! Ha!
—God
See! God has no sense of humor
—Lucifer

Sudden prayers
make God jump!

If Jesus had wanted
us to be metric he
would have had *ten*
apostles

Prepare to meet thy God
(Jacket & tie. No jeans)

God is not dead.
He's just off on
another project.

GOD *IS* WITH YOU!
(He's just trying to find
someplace to park)

The trouble with God
is He thinks He's
William F. Buckley

I've changed my mind.
To hell with the meek.
—God

JESUS SAVES!
(Save yourself. I'm tired)

As God is my witness
I am innocent!
Let's see if He makes
it to the trial!

If God doesn't believe
in enemas, then why did
He create Toledo?

IN A WORD

Synonym/Antonym Blocks

In each of the blocks below there are four scrambled words. For each word there is an antonym and a synonym in that same block.

Each set of parallel lines in a block contains a pair of antonyms. In Block A, for example, the two horizontal lines contain the words VIVID and DINGY. The two vertical lines also contain words that are opposite in meaning to each other.

Just to make it interesting, each block also contains two synonyms, but these are always perpendicular to each other. For example, in Block A, the word BRIGHT is perpendicular to the word VIVID.

Your task is to unscramble the words in all the blocks, making certain you have two synonyms and two antonyms in each.

You must use each letter in a rectangle *once*, except for the corner letters, which are used twice.

A

I	I	V	V	D
R				O
T				C
H				U
B				L
G	D	N	I	Y

B

E	E	A	S	T
S				P
O				R
H				S
O				E
T	Q	I	U	E

C

E	L	M	B	A
B				P
K				I
R				S
U				E
E	H	E	C	R

D

T	C	N	A	S
L				S
N				E
Y				R
E				P
P	M	E	L	A

E

H	U	G	O	R
M				O
O				S
O				A
T				C
S	K	E	L	E

F

L	Y	D	I	E
P				T
E				P
M				M
C				I
O	F	E	C	R

Great Moments in the John—And Not So Great

Charles V (1500–1558), Holy Roman Emperor, and King of Spain, was born in the john.

As though George Armstrong Custer hasn't enough problems with his historical legacy, the world's first solar-powered toilet was installed at Custer Battlefield, in Montana, in 1979.

His Holiness Gregory I (590–604) recommended the toilet as an ideal place to read and have serious thought.

During the American War of Independence, Benjamin P. Ainsworth of Philadelphia offered china commodes with a picture of George III of England painted on the inside bottom.

Queen Elizabeth I (1533–1603), after attending a demonstration of a crude working model of a flush toilet system, declared it an instrument of the devil (effectively ending bathroom research for several hundred years).

Elvis Presley, Lenny Bruce and George II of England all died in the john.

Queen Anne (1665–1714) of England suffered a bad gash when the royal commode collapsed under her. Her new model had a marble seat.

Henry IV (1367–1413) of England survived an assassination attempt in the john because he liked to take passengers along with him to hold discussions.

James I (1394–1437) of Scotland was murdered in the john. So was Henry III (1551–1589) of France and the Roman emperor Heliogabalus (204–222).

Trifles and Tangents

Who Said. . . ?

It's interesting to note that W.C. Fields did not say "Anybody who hates children and dogs can't be all that bad," and that the Bible does not say "Cleanliness is next to godliness." (It was John Wesley in "On Dress: Sermon No. 93.") But most of the following statements should be familiar. Who said:

1. "Never look back—someone might be gaining on you."

2. "One of these days, Alice, pow! Right on the kisser!"

3. "On King! On, you huskies!"

4. "Frankly, my dear, I don't give a damn."

5. These short phrases have become part of the world's vocabulary because of their popularity. Who made them famous?

   a. "I don't get no respect."

   b. "Now cut that out!"

   c. "I kid you not."

6. These were famous company slogans. Whose?

   a. Cover the Earth

   b. The Flavor Lasts

   c. Soft, Strong, Pops Up Too

   d. When better cars are built, ________ will build them

7. It doesn't matter if you get these. Just treasure them.

   a. When told that President Coolidge had died she said:
   "How can they tell?"
   Kate Hepburn? Dorothy Parker? Edna Ferber?

   b. To a barber, when asked how he would like his hair cut, this man replied, "In perfect silence."
   George S. Kaufman? Robert Benchley? Somerset Maugham?

   c. A budding musician forced himself upon this great composer asking that he listen to, and evaluate, two original compositions. After the young man had played one, the composer said, "You need not play any more. I prefer the other one."
   Rossini? Verdi? Hindemith?

Diverting Articles

Triskaidekaphobia

No one really knows for sure how triskaidekaphobia got started, but morbid fear of the number 13 is real enough, and certainly popular. Although it does not seem to be as emotionally based as, say, nyctophobia (morbid fear of night) or astrophobia (thunder and lightning) or even ailurophobia (cats), triskaidekaphobia nevertheless has a grip on our consciousness.

It's almost automatic, for example, for all high-rise buildings, especially hotels, to simply avoid labeling any floor *13*. In Paris, a *quatorzième*, a professional guest, can be hired on the spur of the moment to bring a dinner party up to 14. Then there's the media penchant for pointing out the ironic coincidences involving the number 13. We were reminded on all television networks during the Cuban missile crisis of 1962 that it had lasted 13 days. At NASA, the Apollo 13 space mission was to be launched in April 1970 at 1313 hours central standard time, from pad 39 (3 × 13). Real devotees of triskaidekaphobia pointed out before the launch that the first names of the Apollo 13 astronauts (James, Fred, and John) had a total of 13 letters, and even objected to the fact that their rest periods were scheduled for 13 minutes after the hour.

It could be that the triskaidekaphobic objectors had a legitimate fear. Or maybe it was coincidence. But during the flight, on April 13, an oxygen tank exploded on the space craft, and the mission had to be aborted. The NASA administration building, incidentally, does have a floor 13.

No one seemed more besieged by the number 13 than composer Richard Wagner. Indeed it may even explain his apparent obsession with the dark side of things. Wagner was born in 1813 and died on February 13, 1883. At the age of 13, his mother and sisters moved to Prague, leaving him behind at school in Dresden.

Only 13 of Wagner's operas survive in complete form, because he destroyed a lot of his work, not least his very first opera which premiered on February 13, 1838, to a resounding lack of enthusiasm. *Tannhauser* was completed on April 13, 1845, and its premiere, too, was somewhat of a bomb. The revision, premiered on March 13, 1861, in Paris, was a critical disaster.

But Wagner is not the only well-known name to bring up stories of the number 13. Franklin Delano Roosevelt was plagued by triskaidekaphobia and would not sit at a luncheon table or attend a dinner party if there were 13 people. King Arthur—and we all know what happened to the Round Table—had twelve chief knights sitting there with him. The Last Supper, with Jesus and the twelve apostles, makes an obvious number. There is a long-standing conviction that it is the Last Supper that gave birth to the obsession with 13. But a story from Norse mythology, much older than the time of Christ, tells how Loki the god of evil crashed a party and brought the ranks to 13, shortly after which disaster ensued.

One of the most curious stories of the number 13 comes from the autobiography of Harry Furniss, a caricaturist for *Punch* magazine and member of the London Thirteen Club. Furniss published a letter he received in 1894, from Christiania, Norway.

> Sir—I see you are going to have an anniversary dinner on the 13th of this month, and I take the liberty to send you the following: In 1873, March 20th, I left Liverpool on the steamship *Atlantic*, then bound for New York. On the 13th day, the 1st of April, we went on the rocks near Halifax, Nova Scotia. Out of nearly 1,000 human beings, 580 died.
>
> The first day out from Liverpool some ladies at my table discovered that we were thirteen, and in their consternation requested their gentlemen-companion to move to another table. Out of the entire thirteen, I was the only one who was saved. I was asked at the time if I did not believe in the unlucky number 13. I told them I did not. In this case the believers were all lost and the unbeliever saved.
>
> (Signed) N. Brandt.

Absolutely Indispensable Trivia

Up to c. 480 BC the sculptors of ancient Greece created all testicles equal on their statues of male figures. After this time, however, the pattern changed so that the right testicle was always smaller and higher.

In the first ever Tarzan movie, starring Elmo Lincoln, the monkeys were played by football players from the New Orleans Athletic Club. Only the lion was real. But Lincoln killed it when its sedative wore off during the filming and it jumped him.

The first ever TV commercial in the United States was for Bulova watches. It aired in 1941 on WNBT, New York, and cost Bulova nine dollars.

The standard length of the axle on Roman chariots was 143.5 cm or 4 feet, 8½ inches, the same as North American railroad tracks.

In April 1984, the Hundred Years War (1338–1453) was surpassed as the longest ever recorded war. Although Liechtenstein disbanded its army in 1868, a clerical oversight has allowed the country to remain at war with Prussia ever since.

Shortly after the publication of *Les Miserables*, Victor Hugo wrote to his publishers, Hurst and Blackett, to inquire how it was selling.
Hugo's letter was simply: "?"
The reply: "!"

The three-toed sloth has six more ribs than an elephant.

visuthink

1. This is a polygon. (Actually it's an octagon.) Not that it matters what you call it, but we're tired of "figure" and "diagram."

   How many more lines would be necessary if you were to join each letter to every other letter? (If this takes you more than a minute, you're in trouble!)

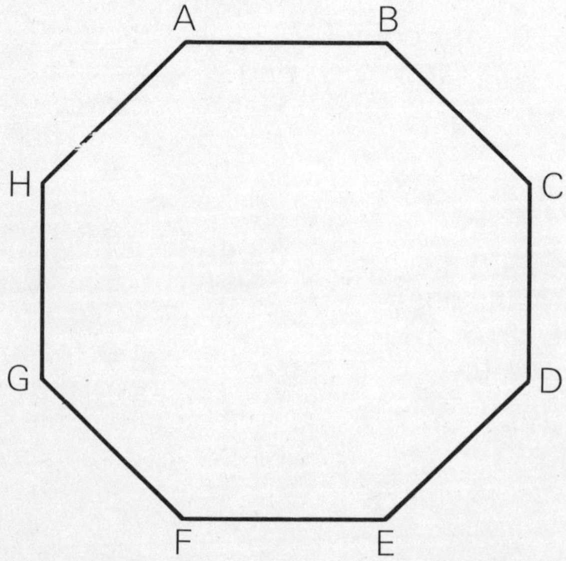

2. Is there something wrong with any of these cards?

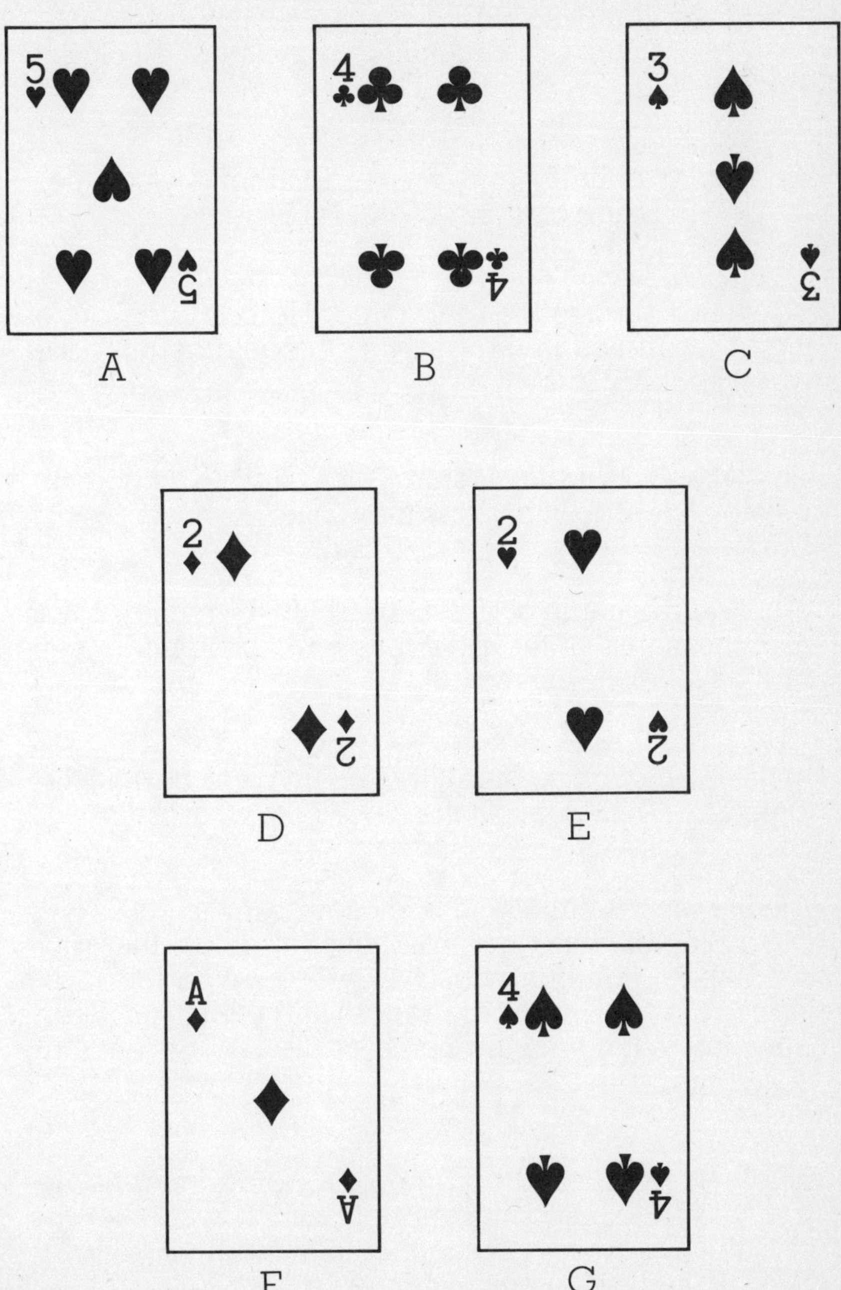

Trifles and Tangents

"Black is the color of my true love's hair." It was also the color of Dick Turpin's horse (Black Bess) and Babe Ruth's bat (Black Betsy). See if you can handle some more blackness, below.

1. A popular country and western singer always performed in black clothing. What is his name?

2. Edward Teach is his real name. He operated out of the West Indies in the early eighteenth century. He was popularly known as?

3. The Black Rebels Motorcycle Club was led by Marlon Brando. What was the movie?

4. This was the name of U.S. General J.J. Pershing. It was also the name of the riderless horse at John F. Kennedy's funeral.

5. In the Black Sox scandal (the 1919 World Series), the Chicago White Sox lost the series. To what team?

6. A very successful comic book series in the 1950s was "The Blackhawks," an international group that traveled about fighting evil. They were seven men with names like Andre (from France) and Olaf (from Scandinavia). What was the name of the short, stout Chinese man?

7. Black Beauty was the name of a horse in Anna Sewell's wonderful children's classic. It was also the name of a radio hero's car (a Lincoln Zephyr, incidentally). Who was this radio crime fighter?

8. On the television series *Gunsmoke*, this man played a continuing minor role as Dodge City's part-Indian blacksmith. When he left the series he became a very famous movie star. Who?

9. True or false: The black snake is non-poisonous?

10. His surname was Plantagenet, and he was known as the Black Prince. What was his first name?

11. During what war did the Black Hole of Calcutta incident take place?
a. The Seven Years War b. The Hundred Years War
c. The Sepoy Rebellion d. The Boer War.

12. The Black Hand is a society that originated in Sicily in the nineteenth century. The Blackfoot are a group of Indian peoples of the North American plains. A black body is something that presumably absorbs all of the energy near it and reflects none. What is blackleg?

Contemplator's Corner

More Puzzles without a Pencil

1. A lighthouse keeper is preparing to take a bath in his modern, airtight, windowless bathroom. Suddenly the door slams shut, the door knob falls off and he's trapped. In a panic he turns the water off and breaks off the tap. Water gushes out of the pipe, overflows the tub, and soon begins to fill the room. The keeper is desperate. He can't get out, he can't stop the water from coming in. How will he keep from drowning?

2. Another incorrect equation. You can correct it by moving *one* of the sticks.

VI – IV = IX

3. Jack's mother promised to quit smoking as soon as she finished the sixteen cigarettes left in her pack. But like any normal addict, she found she could extend the process by rolling four butts into yet one more cigarette. How many cigarettes did she manage to get before finally quitting?

4. The letters G, H, R and X are missing from this alphabet. Should they go above or below the line?

```
A    EF    I KLMN        T VW  YZ
_________________________________
 BCD       J       OPQ  S U
```

ICE-BREAKERS

More Absolutely Indispensable Trivia

Not until 1920 did the projected life expectancy of human beings in the Western World surpass that of goldfish. (Living in their wild state, the expectancy is 50 years. Human life expectancy at the end of World War I was 48.4 years.)

In 1976, for the first time, all the Nobel Prizes went to one country: the United States. This was also a year, however, in which no prize for Peace was awarded.

The undisputed symbol and star of beach party and surfing movies in the 1960s was teenage rock 'n roll idol Frankie Avalon. He starred in six of these box office successes. Frankie Avalon cannot swim.

Ben Jonson is buried upright in Westminster Abbey to preserve space. He is the only one to be buried in that fashion. His epitaph: "O rare Ben Jonson."

Henry Ford's first automobile had no reverse gear.

Pope Eugenius III arrived in Paris, France, on a Friday in the year 1147. Friday was a day of fast and abstinence, but the arrival of His Holiness was an occasion for feasting and celebration. The pope therefore issued a decree declaring Friday a Thursday so the populace could have a party.

The most unsuccessful animal rescue ever, took place on January 14, 1978, when volunteers from the British army, filling in for striking firemen, were called by an elderly lady in South London to get her cat out of a tree. They extricated the cat with no difficulty whatever, and then ran over it as they drove back to the station.

The Case of the Prolific Mule

Judge Harvey Bottrell squinted over the edge of his long, polished bench. He did not know whether to appear stern or amused. Before him stood a slight, dapper man whose face, like the judge's, seemed ready to switch from sheepishness to confidence and back again.

"T.A. Jones," Judge Bottrell said. "T.A. Jones. What is this, the fifth time you've been in my court? When are you going to stop? What did you do this time? Sell some poor sucker the Panama Canal?"

T.A. Jones smiled up at the judge. "I don't know why I'm here, your honor." He turned slightly to involve the court clerk in his next statement. "This is a perfectly straight business deal. It's just those guys in the bunco squad at 42 Division. Y'know, Har—your honor, I think they've got it in for me. I'm just an average guy trying to make a buck and—"

"Sure. Average." Judge Bottrell picked up his gavel and pointed it at Jones. "Like the interview-tape series made at President Kennedy's funeral. You interviewed famous people about Kennedy and sold the tapes to radio stations. Let's see now. You had an interview with Eva Peron. There was Ernest Hemingway, Clark Gable, Pius XII."

Jones' face brightened. "Y'know, your honor. Those tapes ran on over forty stations. Think of the history I gave to children. Think—"

"I suppose you were teaching history in your Fraternal Biography series too," the judge interrupted. "Biographies written by the brother or sister of a famous person. 'Provides Intimate Details No One Else Would Know.' Wasn't that the slogan? Let's see. You had Elton John's biography. One for Robert Louis Stevenson, Eleanor Roosevelt, Frank Sinatra. There were more, but I forget."

Jones' eyes misted a little. "Yea, that was a good one." The court clerk looked up at Judge Bottrell. "The royal boxes," he whispered.

The judge nodded. "Do you still have any royal jewelry boxes, Mr. Jones? The ones inscribed George I and Nicholas I. You had a Leopold I of Belgium too, as I recall."

"Well, they *were* attractive pieces, though." Jones' sheepish look was returning. "And I only sold one of each. After all, it wasn't as though I mass-produced George I's personal jewelry box. In fact—"

The judge cut him off. "I think this one today is one of your worst—or best." He smiled to himself. "Shares in the next foals out of Tarbottom's Lady."

"But look, Har—your honor." Jones held out both his hands. "Tarbottom's Lady is a real honest-to-goodness mule—no ordinary one either. This mule has won the dead-weight pulling contest at Regina, at Tulsa, in Calgary at the Stampede. And that's only this year. She's incredible. No mule has ever pulled this much. And I've got proof."

Judge Bottrell looked at the court clerk, who nodded enthusiastically and held up several photographs and newspaper clippings.

T.A. Jones meanwhile was getting very warmed up. "All I'm doing is selling shares in her next foals. It's done all the time with race horses. Even with cattle. Why not mules?"

The court clerk was still nodding at the judge.

"T.A. Jones, you're something else," the judge said. "I have half a mind to let you go. Anyone who buys shares probably deserves them. You might even start with my clerk here."

What does Judge Bottrell know that apparently the clerk does not? Can you explain T.A. Jones' other frauds?

Trifles and Tangents

Name that Name

Gunslinger Wild Bill Hickok (1837–1876) may have been known as "Wild Bill," but his real name was James Butler Hickok. As a boy, his very long nose and protruding upper lip got him the nickname "Duck Bill." It is not difficult to see why he encouraged the change.

Butch Cassidy's real name was George LeRoy Parker. The Sundance Kid's name was Harry Longabaugh. Everyone knows Billy the Kid as William H. Bonney, but he was born Henry McCarty. And then there was Calamity Jane who was Martha Jane Canary.

Confused? Try these.

For one reason or another each of the following lists has a name in it that does not belong. If you can identify something common to the group, it should be easy to weed out the extra one.

Warm ups

1. Sleepy
   Dopey
   Happy
   Bashful
   Doc
   Smiley
   Grumpy
   Sneezy

2. Patti
   Doris
   LaVerne
   Maxene

3. Washington Capitals
   Calgary Flames
   Seattle Mariners
   Vancouver Canucks
   Quebec Nordiques

4. Gioacchino Rossini
   Edward Elgar
   Franz Josef Haydn
   Karl Ditters von Dittersdorf
   Eugenio Pacelli

Just a little tougher

5. Pappy Yokum, Daisy Mae Scraggs, Lena the Hyena, Moonbeam McSwine, Lemuel Leaver

6. Danube, Po, Madeira, Elbe, Tiber

7. Ham, Shadrach, Shem, Japheth

8. Queensland, New South Wales, Perth, Victoria

Now if you can get these, you're really good

9. Davis, Dwight Filley
   Nelson, Oswald George
   Stanley, Frederick Arthur
   Grey, Albert Henry George

10. Gaston and Louis
Horace and John
August and Frederick
Donald and Phil

11. Martin Zarcovich
Patrick Garrett
Henri Dunant
John Selman
Robert Ford

You'll get this one but will you know why?

12. Somerset Maugham
Ernest Hemingway
e.e. cummings
Girolamo Fracastoro (1483–1553)

The Academic Snob Graffiti Page

Point of view is relative
(SAID PICASSO TO EINSTEIN)

Descartes thought he was here

Sisyphus was a pusher

Agnes was a morning person.
JOHN KEATS

I told them at Buick,
It'll never fly.
PERCY SHELLEY

Observing the glanded
gentry is exhausting.
D.H. LAWRENCE

Gordian is at loose
ends.
ALEXANDER

Schroedinger rules the
waves!

Tutankhamen has
changed his mind. He
wants to be buried at sea.

Roman mythology
is redundant

I am oxymoronic
even when I am not

Von Karajan can't tell his
brass from his oboe

Back in a minute.
GODOT

Tolkien is hobbit forming

Emmanuel Kant
but Genghis Khan

T.S. Eliot is an
anagram for toilets

Diverting Articles

There is No Greater Fate than Coincidence

At 12:36 p.m., on July 20, 1944, Colonel Claus Count von Stauffenberg excused himself from the conference table at Hitler's Wolfschanze headquarters in East Prussia. He explained to the officer next to him that he had an important telephone call to make. On the floor, in von Stauffenberg's briefcase, was the bomb that had just been triggered to eliminate Adolf Hitler six minutes later. The Count had sat to one side of Hitler and the briefcase was now only a few feet away from the Führer's legs. But then—coincidence? destiny? control by some force greater than us all? or just bad luck?—when von Stauffenberg left, the officer he had spoken to moved the briefcase to give himself more room. He put it behind a heavy table support, away from his legs—and from Hitler. The bomb exploded with devastating effect, but certainly not the effect intended.

Forty-three years earlier, but not too far away, coincidence, or fate, or destiny, was busy again, this time in what should have been the first powered flight by an aircraft. On Lake Tullnerback in Austria, on a warm October morning in 1901, a young piano-maker, William Kress, was attempting to take off in an aircraft that essentially matched many of the specifications that the Wright brothers were to use successfully only two years later. It should have flown. It didn't. Unknown to Kress, the Mercedes engine shipped to him was the wrong size. He had ordered a 500-pound engine that would deliver 40HP. The one he got was too heavy and the nose of the aircraft would not lift.

Human error? Perhaps. Or maybe human weakness. That certainly is one way to explain the myriad of coincidences that govern not only history but also our personal lives. Certainly human weakness might account for a degree of fate in the outcome of the Battle of Waterloo. Contemporary accounts of Napoleon's hemorrhoids explain that he was too uncomfortable to sit on his horse that day because of the condition. Since Napoleon, who was very short in stature, customarily sat on his horse for a better view of the battlefield, is it illogical to wonder whether Napoleon's piles shaped the outcome of the battle?

But weakness can only account partially for other phenomena: the case of the famous ghost ship *Mary Celeste*, for example. The story of how she was found abandoned but intact off Portugal in December 1872 is well known. But this is only part of her mystery. Two days after she first slid into the Atlantic in 1861 (christened *The Amazon*, by the way) her captain died. Her second captain was fired. The third rammed another ship in the Dover Straits, and the fourth ran her aground on Cape Breton. She was then abandoned, but salvaged again in 1867. Her new owner went bankrupt. Under yet another owner, the famous incident took place. The next owner sent her to Uruguay in 1873 and she lost most of her cargo in a storm. On the return journey the cargo (horses) *and* the captain died. In 1884 she was sold again, ran into a reef off Haiti, and burned to the waterline.

Was the *Mary Celeste* jinxed. Or is her history a legacy of unfortunate human weakness? Either way, bad luck is bad luck, no matter how one analyzes it. At least the people of Peshtigo, Wisconsin, would agree. On the night of October 8, 1871, a forest fire burned their whole town completely to the ground, with a dreadful loss of 1,500 lives. The community had only 2,000 people. Yet they got no publicity and, as a result, almost no relief or government aid. Why? October 8, 1871, was also the night of the famous Chicago fire, which everyone knows about even though in comparison with Peshtigo's it was a conflagration of minor proportions.

No doubt one of the reasons why fate is so much more attractive than the notion of simple coincidence is that much of the analysis about it is done by hindsight. The elements that bring two events together invariably contain fascinating possibilities and these are easy to search out, after the fact. Take the famous comparison of John F. Kennedy's assassination and that of Abraham Lincoln's. Both presidents were civil rights leaders; both suffered fatal head wounds; both were slain in front of their wives. Both were succeeded by southern Democrat senators named Johnson. Both assassins were slain before going to trial. Booth shot Lincoln in a theater and ran into a warehouse. Oswald shot Kennedy from a warehouse and ran into a theater. Booth was born in 1839, Oswald in 1939. Lincoln's secretary, named Kennedy, advised against going to the theater. Kennedy's secretary—yes, named Lincoln—urged against the open car in Dallas. The list is even greater if one starts to count things like the number of letters in the names of the principals.

Yet, to stretch hindsight to its conclusions, it is easy to find an entire catalogue of differences between the Kennedy and

Lincoln situations. (One of the most interesting is that Lincoln's son, Robert Todd Lincoln, was present at his father's murder, at that of James Garfield, and of William McKinley. He was not, for obvious reasons, at Kennedy's.)

Undeniably, hindsight, and the careful sifting of information, can make coincidence more powerful. Yet the pull toward a belief that there is a "divinity that shapes our ends" is irresistible. On the same day, June 28, 1914, that Crown Prince Ferdinand was shot in Sarajevo (the motorcade route had been changed to foil assassins, but coincidentally, nobody had told Ferdinand's chauffeur), a Siberian peasant woman had tried to kill Gregory Rasputin in Tobolsk. She failed to dispatch the mysterious monk. On the other hand, Ferdinand's assassin was terrifyingly successful. What would the world be like today if the outcome of the two incidents had been reversed?

IN A WORD

Roundhouse Words

Each of the circles below has a word that can be spelled out by starting at the right letter and following around the circle in a clockwise direction until the word is determined. For example, the following circle spells TILT:

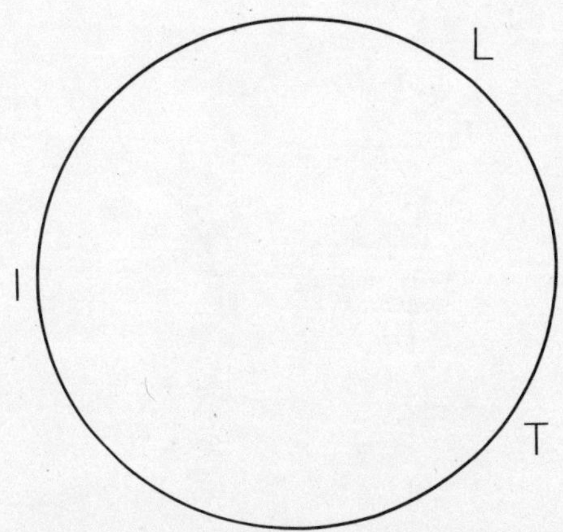

1.

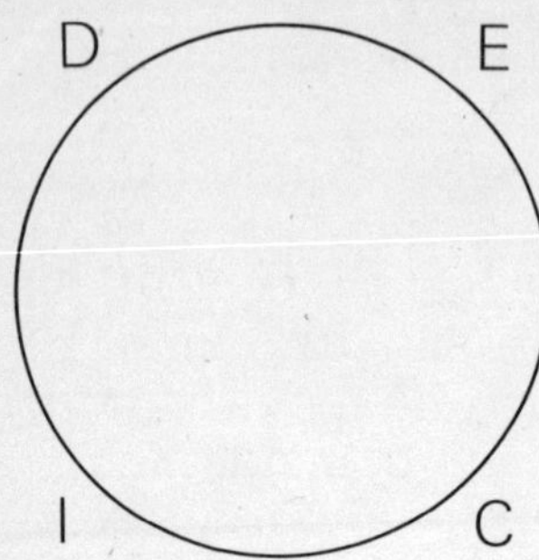

2.

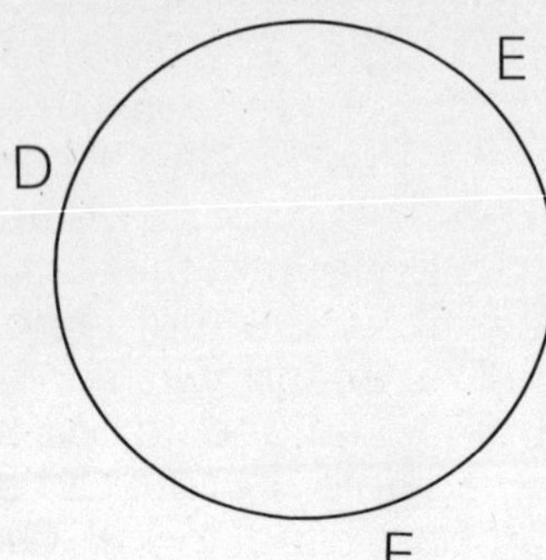

3.

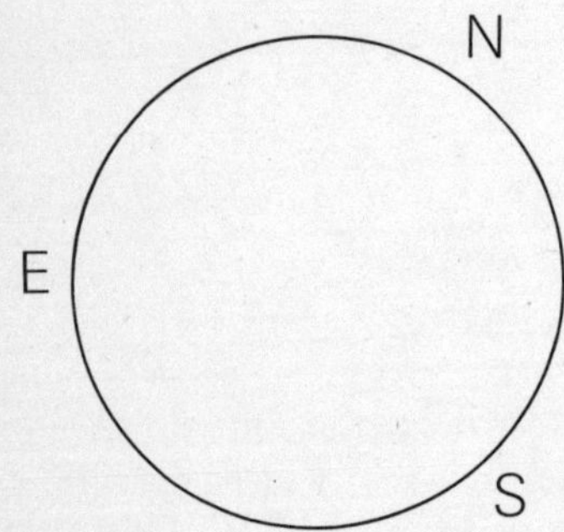

4.

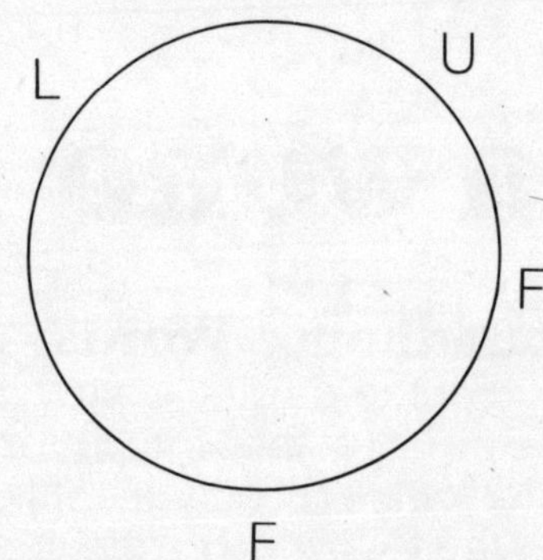

5.

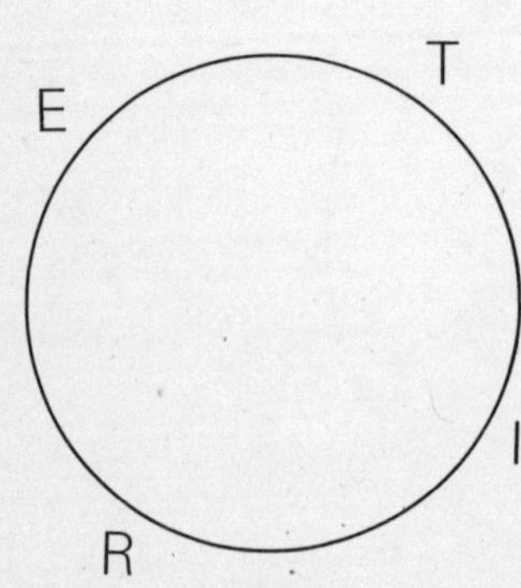

6.

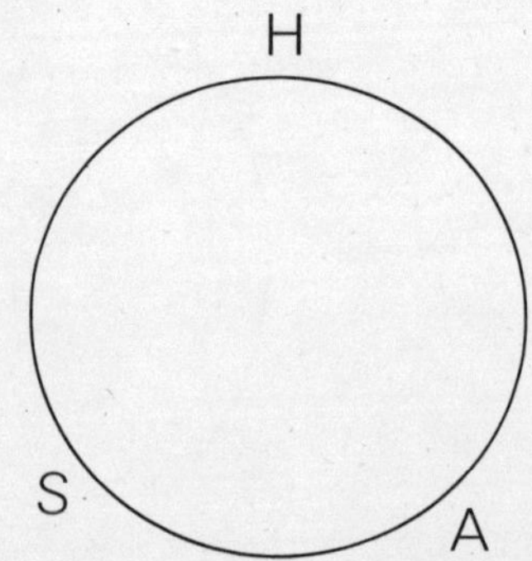

7.

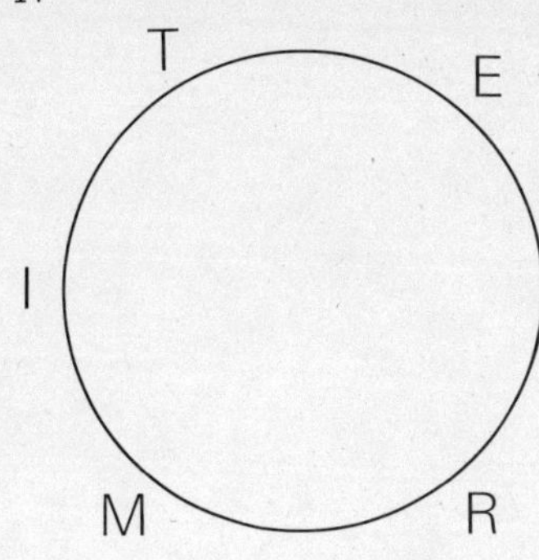

8.

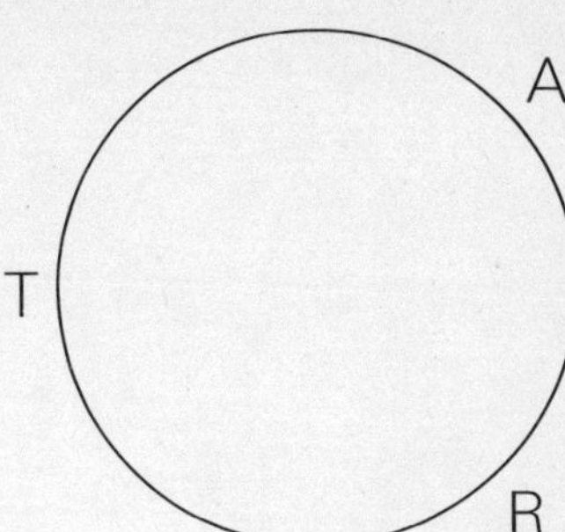

9.

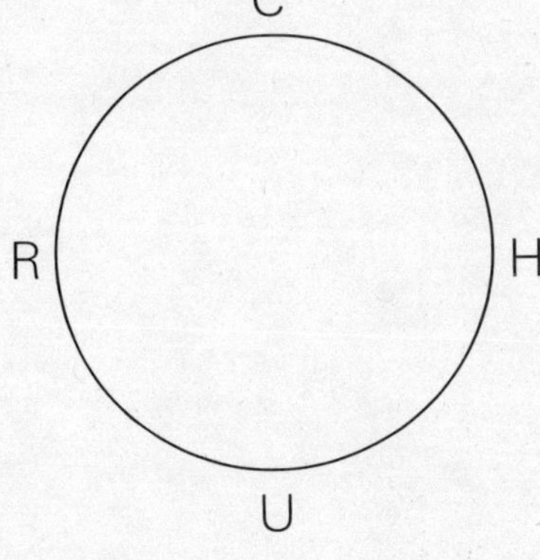

10.

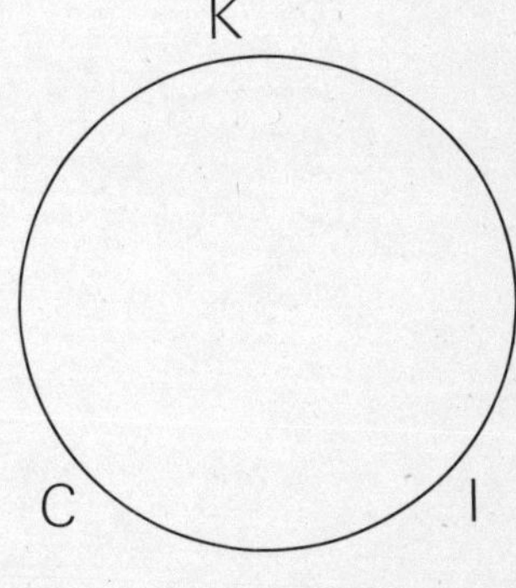

11.

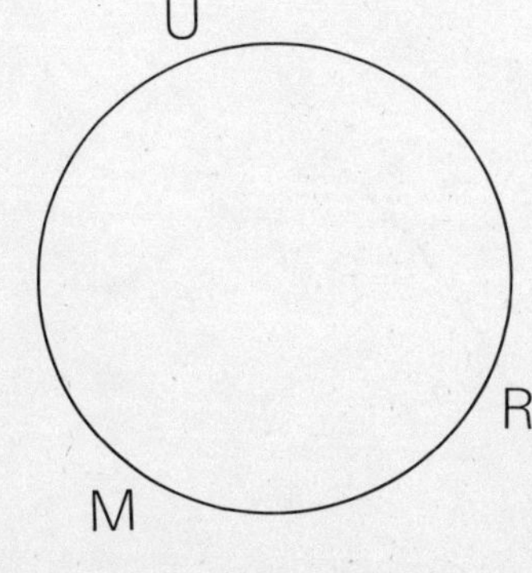

12.

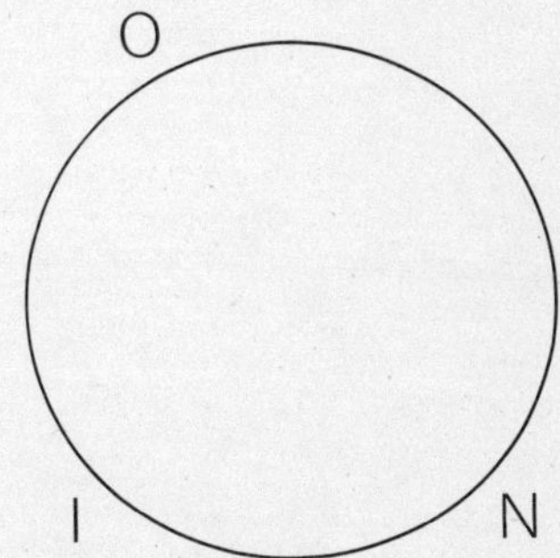

13.

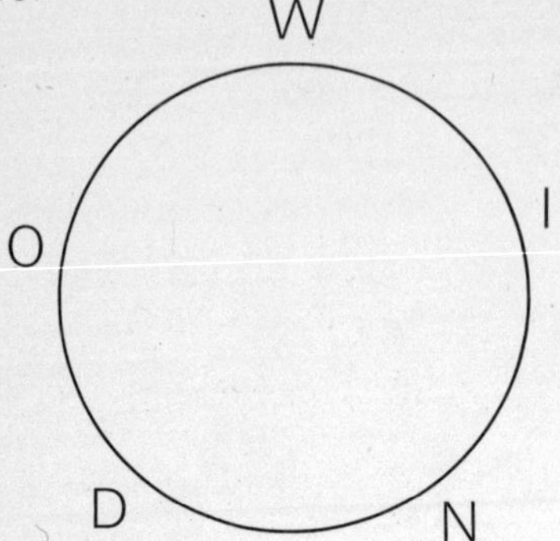

14.

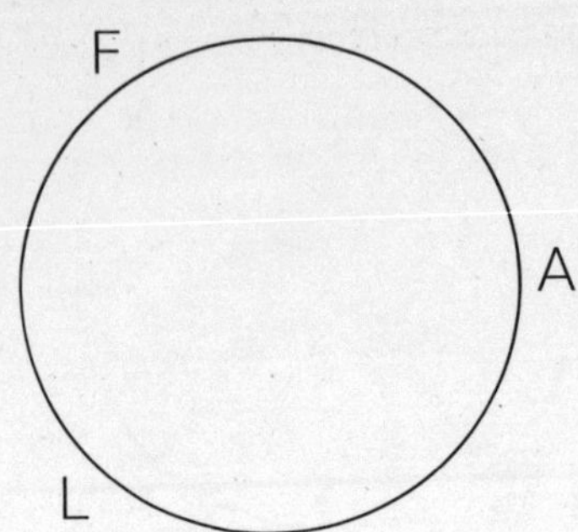

15.

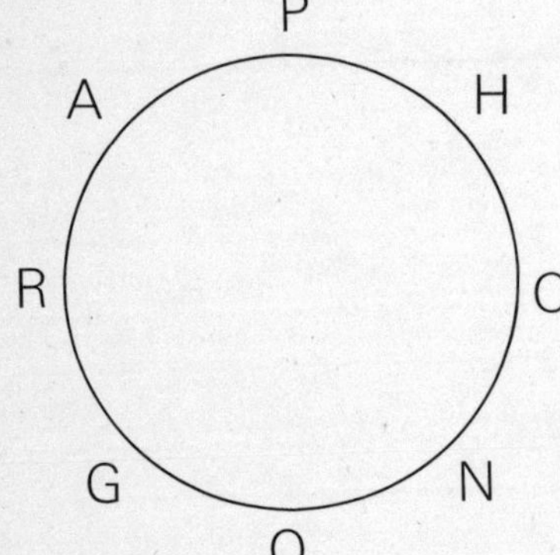

Trifles and Tangents

Musically Speaking

The American publishing rights to Handel's *Messiah* were long held by the Westman Publishing Company. In 1923, they successfully sued the composers of "Yes, We Have No Bananas" for copyright violation, claiming that the song was stolen from the opening bars of the Hallelujah Chorus.

Now, we didn't expect you to know that, but there are some other wonderful things about music and composers that you might know.

1. Match the first names and last names of these composers. You may know them by three names—for example, Franz Josef Haydn, instead of Franz Haydn. But that's too easy. Here we just have the *first* name and the surname.

	Surname	**First Name**
a.	Handel	Alexander
b.	Bach	Nikolai
c.	Copeland	Karl
d.	Scriabin	Modest
e.	Kreisler	Arthur
f.	Sullivan	Aaron
g.	Mozart	Johannes
h.	Rimski-Korsakov	Johann
i.	Brahms	George
j.	Mussorsky	Fritz

2. In what section of a symphony orchestra would you find each of these groups of instruments?

a.	*b.*	*c.*
castanets	oboe	tuba
triangle	bassoon	trombone
tambourine	clarinet	
glockenspiel		

3. Match the composer and the composition.

Bernstein	The Emperor Concerto
Beethoven	The Young Person's Guide to the Orchestra
Gershwin, Gershwin and Heyward	West Side Story
Rachmaninov	The Life and Times of Joseph Stalin
Britten	Porgy and Bess
Wilson	Rhapsody on a Theme of Paganini

Contemplator's Corner

More No-Pencil Puzzles

1. Steve Fleck drove from Winnipeg to Chicago with his family. They shared the driving and made the trip in one span, without stopping to rest. The journey took hours, and for the entire time the car had a flat tire, which they never bothered to repair. How is this possible?

2. How often can you subtract the numeral 1.0 from the numeral 21.5?

3. If you had to repair this 24 carat gold bracelet at a cost of $10 per link cut, and $50 per link welded, how could you make it one continuous chain for $180?

4. Imagine 3 horizontal lines, a centimetre apart, one above the other. Now imagine 3 vertical lines, a centimetre apart, cutting through the horizontal lines. How many squares have been formed? No pencil, remember!

SHERLOCK of the John

The Case at 247 Hanover Street

As he pulled over to the curb, Chief Struan Ritchie cocked his head a little more attentively toward the car radio.

"The wettest first day of October since records were started in 1844," the weather forecaster was saying, "and the outlook for the next few weeks doesn't promise anything better either. More of the sa—"

Ritchie snapped off the radio, and looked gloomily across the sidewalk at 247 Hanover Street. A perfectly miserable day for a perfectly miserable case.

"And come to think of it"—he was talking out loud to himself now—"a perfectly miserable place for it too."

Indeed, 247 Hanover Street was more forbidding than inviting. Although the brick pillars and wrought iron fence would not have kept out any serious intruder, they spoke "unwelcome" most eloquently. And if that failed, the heavy double doors under a poorly lit portico repeated the suggestion that 247 Hanover Street in Halifax was not a place one came to unnecessarily.

The Chief grunted audibly, as he heaved himself out of his car. He stared at the house again for a second or two and then walked over to an empty squad car, opened the door and turned off the flashing red roof-lights. As he moved uncomfortably toward the house, the rain began to pelt down again, and he ran the last few steps.

Inside, the scene took his mind off the weather and his developing foul mood. Two of his officers stood over the body of Quentin Barrow III. It was obvious that Barrow was not going to be bothered by all the people in his house. One of the policemen, the younger one, almost stood to attention as he spoke.

"We were first on, sir! Nothing's been touched. The lab has been called. We've got three possibles in the next room."

Ritchie frowned. "Three possibles?"

"Yes, sir! The daughter, the handyman, and the butler."

Ritchie's frown deepened.

"No sir! No butler jokes." This time the other officer was speaking. "I think he's really a kind of valet anyway, but he said 'butler.' Anyway he has an alibi. They all do. I mean, you can tell by your nose that Barrow's been dead for at least a day or more and he—the butler I mean—he's been off for the last week. Got a Vancouver hotel receipt for September 24 through the 31st to prove it."

"And the others?" Chief Ritchie wanted to know.

"Well the daughter, she is like—uh—well it's pretty iron-clad, sir."

The partner spoke up. "She's been drying out for a week, sir. Just got out of the hospital. Came home this afternoon and saw the butler standing out in the portico. It seems neither of them had a key so they sent for the handyman. He lives across town."

"And what's *his* alibi?" the Chief asked.

"Well, he only comes here once a week. Tomorrow's his day, and he missed last week. He says his wife can back it up. Probably can too, for what it's worth. It all looks like a dead end to me."

"I'm not so sure," Ritchie replied. "I think the first thing we'll do is call that Vancouver hotel."

What had Chief Ritchie noticed that the patrolman had missed?

ICE-BREAKERS

Still More Absolutely Indispensable Trivia

Florence Nightingale, throughout her tenure as a nurse in the Crimea, carried a live owl in her pocket.

Sound waves from vowels in our language have over 600 times the force of most consonants.

The Virgin Mary has appeared on the cover of *Time* magazine more often than any other woman.

In 1911, Robert Leech successfully rode over Niagara Falls in a barrel. Some years later he slipped on a banana peel and died of complications from the fall.

Henry VIII of England lost the famous "Jesus Bells" of St. Paul's to Sir Miles Partridge in a dice game. Foolishly, Partridge collected. When he was hanged for a "criminal" offense a few years later, the bells were rung throughout the execution ceremony.

The knuckle joints in your hand are lubricated by fluid that contains tiny gas bubbles. When your knuckles "pop," it is these tiny bubbles exploding.

In 1892, the Coca Cola company stopped advertising coke as a medicinal compound and began to urge it on the public as a pause that refreshes.

Standing for the national anthem was a practice that did not become widespread until World War I.

Trifles and Tangents

Great Dates

It's interesting—alarming to some—to think that if the International World Calendar Association does not have its way, the times will be truly out of joint by the year 2000. It's all because the earth goes around the sun every 365.2422 days, and even our leap year doesn't quite account for that .2422 of a day. So by AD 2000 our calendar will be seriously out of whack. But even so serious a problem should not keep you from answering these.

1. Match the event with its correct year.

a. Korean war ends in truce	1958
b. U-2 shot down over Russia	1572
c. Napoleon Bonaparte dies	1564
d. General James Wolfe dies on Plains of Abraham	1905
e. Josef Stalin dies	1821
f. The Saint Bartholomew's Day Massacre	1501
g. Henry VIII's older brother (Arthur) marries Catharine of Aragon	1953
h. William Shakespeare is born	1759
i. Admiral Togo of Japan destroys Russian Baltic fleet	1649
j. Charles I of England executed	1960

2. Why do people—or perhaps, why *should* they—remember these dates?
   - *a.* June 6, 1944
   - *b.* July 20, 1969
   - *c.* September 3 to 13, 1752
   - *d.* October 23, 4004 BC
   - *e.* March 15, 44 BC
   - *f.* July 20, 1944

3. How close can you get?

Within twenty years, can you name the year in which:

a. Jonas Salk announced the discovery of his vaccine for polio?

b. Henry Hudson sailed into Hudson's Bay?

c. The Gatling gun (first machine gun) was used in warfare?

d. Johann Gutenberg first used movable metallic type?

Within thirty years can you name the year in which:

e. Sir Alexander Fleming discovered penicillin?

f. Vasco da Gamma first sailed the sea route to India?

g. Nikolaus Otto invented the four-cycle gasoline engine?

h. The world's last dodo bird died on the island of Mauritius?

4. Which came first:

a. The Beatles last public concert, or the capture of the USS *Pueblo* by North Korea?

b. The last married pope ascends the throne in Rome, or Eric the Red discovers Greenland?

c. Albert Einstein publishes the theory of relativity, or Jesse James' brother Frank dies peacefully in his bed?

d. Spermatozoa is first observed under a microscope, or ether is first used as an anesthesia?

5. Since Father Hennepin first looked on Niagara Falls (the first white man to do so), how many years have there been in our calendar that will read the same upside-down and right-side up?

Diverting Articles

"Say it Ain't So, Joe"—But it Was

The 1920 World Series between the Cleveland Indians and the Brooklyn Robins should have been the capper to one of the greatest seasons ever in major league baseball. World War I was well out of the way and both leagues were back at full strength. Babe Ruth, sold to the Yankees by the Boston Red Sox the previous winter, had given up pitching to hit 54 home runs. The American league winners, the Cleveland Indians, were managed by their own centerfielder, Tris Speaker, who had hit a phenomenal .388. The National League's Brooklyn Robins had Leon Cadore who pitched a 26-inning game in May. The series itself saw the first ever World Series grand slam (the Indian's Elmer Smith off spit-baller, Burleigh Grimes); the first ever World Series home run by a pitcher (Jim Bagby); and the first, and so far only, unassisted triple play (by Cleveland second baseman Bill Wambsgamss). It *should* have been the series and the season that everyone talks about. But nothing is ever quite as it should be. The 1920 World Series became noteworthy, primarily because it was believed to be honest.

For almost a year, rumors had been floating about that the World Series the year before had been fixed; that the 1919 contest had been thrown by the Chicago White Sox, who gave it away to the Cincinnati Reds five games to three. Then on September 28, only nine days before the great 1920 Series began, the roof fell in. In response to a newspaper story, Chicago pitcher Eddie Cicotte and famous leftfielder, Shoeless Joe Jackson, confessed that they had taken money to let Cincinnati win. Pitcher Lefty Williams was next to confess, followed by centerfielder Happy Felsch. Before long, first baseman Chick Gandil, shortstop Swede Risberg, and infielders Fred McMullin and Buck Weaver were implicated. Together, they were reported as accepting a bribe of $100,000 to lose to Cincinnati.

The American public was horrorstruck. Impurities in baseball? Never! In boxing or horse racing, sure. And in politics and business—well politics is politics and business is business. But baseball? President Taft in 1910 had called it "the clean, straight game." Teddy Roosevelt praised the "rugged honesty" of baseball players. *The Nation* in 1920 wrote: "We do not trust cashiers. . . or diplomats, or policemen, or physicians, as we trust an outfielder or a shortstop." But now the national game was in disarray and so were the feelings of its supporters.

Newspapers exploded. Coverage was significantly greater than that given the charges of corruption in President Harding's cabinet a few years later. Fans reacted, sometimes violently. On Chicago's south side, a young boy, leader of a White Sox fan club, was beaten because he had championed Swede Risberg. In Joliet, Illinois, Buck Herzog of the Chicago *Cubs* was stabbed by a fan simply because he wore a Chicago uniform.

And the "tainted" players? All eight were immediately suspended by White Sox owner Charles Comiskey (whose role in the revelation of the truth, incidentally, is a morass of contradictions). The Sox were in a dead heat with the Cleveland Indians for the American league pennant in 1920, and this action virtually clinched the pennant for the Indians. All but Fred McMullin were indicted and brought to trial, but the trial smelled as badly as the scandal itself. Most of the gamblers failed to appear. Some were missing; others were "too ill to appear." Written confessions disappeared. Lawyers switched sides. In the end, everyone was acquitted—once more to the disgust of the baseball public.

But in the meantime, the owners had reacted. They reorganized the government of major league baseball and appointed the first Commissioner of Baseball to rule over them. Kenesaw Mountain Landis came in carrying a huge broom. He banned all of the players in the scandal from baseball forever, even Buck Weaver who it was established was not involved in the bribe, although he knew of it. Landis went so far as to threaten the careers of innocent players who had any association whatever with these "Black Sox." For example, White Sox rookie pitcher Dickie Kerr, who was not in on the bribe, had pitched a 3–0 shutout in game three of the 1919 Series despite having five "crooked" players behind him. Yet Landis suspended him for the 1922 season for playing with the accused players in a non-league exhibition game.

How guilty were the Black Sox? Certainly they confessed to involvement, although none got all of the money they were promised. Yet a look at the box scores of the 1919 Series makes one wonder. Joe Jackson's batting average for the series was .375. He had twelve hits, still a record for an eight game series, and he made no errors. Eddie Collins at second base, one of the Clean Sox (or Square Sox, or Opposite Sox as the non-involved players came to be called), had two errors and batted .226. On the other hand, Lefty Williams, a pitcher famous for his control, walked three Reds in a row in the fourth inning of game two, then gave up a triple. Cicotte, an even better control pitcher (29–9 on the year) kept plunking batters. Catcher Ray Schalk, one of the Clean Sox, complained that his signals were being ignored, a strong indication of something wrong. Yet Fred McMullin, one of the banned players, appeared only twice as a pitch-hitter, and went one for two—hardly an example of a dive.

Of course, the biggest legacy of the Black Sox scandal, like all such incidents, is the question: Could it happen today? Not likely, say supporters of major league ball. Salaries, for one thing, are just too good now to risk suspension. And instant TV replay makes it almost impossible to fool anyone. Besides, the great thing about baseball is that every time it stumbles there's always something memorable to pull it up again—like the great 1920 World Series.

IN A WORD

Hiddenhoms

You know that a shoe has a sole of course, and also that sole is a rather tasty type of fish. However, when you are given a clue like "the only part of a shoe that swims," for which the answer is—obviously—*sole*, then *sole* is a "hiddenhom," or hidden homonym. What are the hiddenhoms for these clues?

1. A daily account on the forest floor.
2. A drink that might be used in self-defense.
3. How could you re-string a noise?
4. This would be carrying a dismissal too far.
5. Your landlady needs this for the chess tournament.
6. Morse code weakens but this signal tires.

7. Fish have octaves?

8. Neck-stretching construction equipment.

9. This you get from a horse, or from a duck.

10. If you can't win the rubber with this bid, then use it on your opposition.

11. Exclude the counter.

12. This container was not intended for tender ears.

13. A competitive correspondence? Impossible!

14. Angry from one side all the way to the other.

Contemplator's Corner

1. This is another one of those "if-you're-tired-of-reading" ones. These are fun. If you're a "reader," don't be intimidated. You'll need some equipment: a pencil, a piece of paper and seven coins.

   First, draw this diagram on the paper.

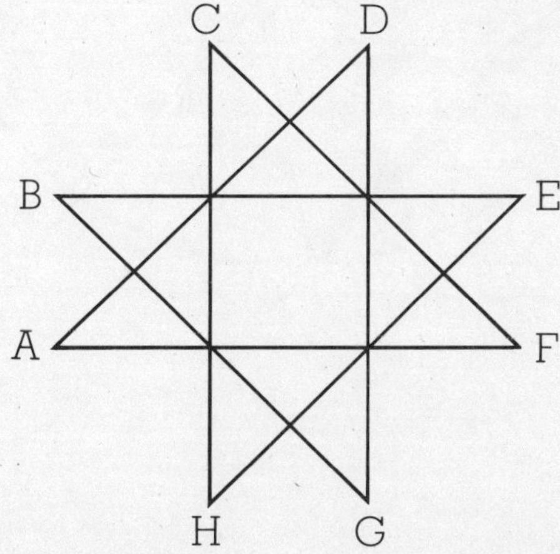

The object is to cover seven of the points on the design with the seven coins, but only by *sliding*. That is, by setting a coin on A, you can (and must) slide it to either D or F.

Once a point is covered, the coin stays there.

You cannot start a slide from a covered point.

2. If you're even too tired to get the equipment you need for the problem above, try this one. You don't have to lift a finger. In fact you *must not* lift a finger.

   Just looking at the diagram, and limiting yourself to ten seconds, how many single sections are there in the circle?

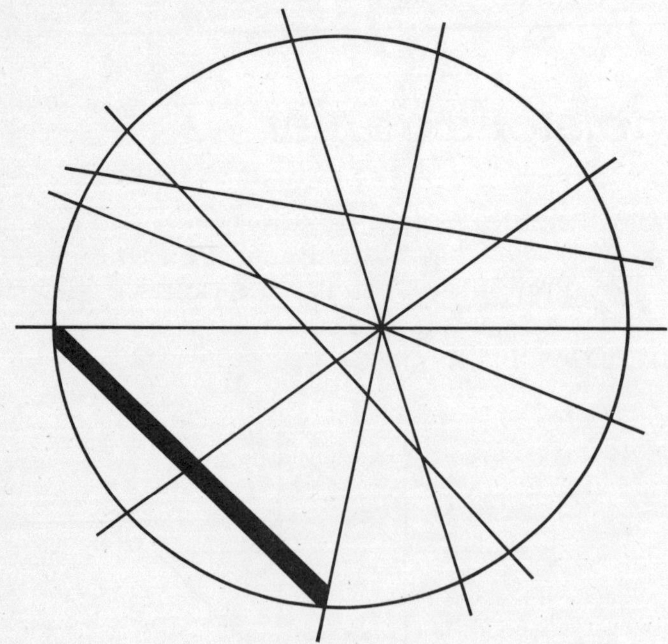

The "Just Too Punny" Graffiti Page

I'd sooner have a bottle in front of
me than a frontal lobotomy

Education kills
by degrees

Keep a balanced outlook,
Vote Sado-Masochist!

You can tell the sex of a
chromosome by taking down
its genes

Would a castrated pig
be disgruntled?

I'd give my right arm
to be ambidextrous

University examinations put
the anal back into analysis

Bad spellers of the world!
Untie!

Perforation is a ripoff

Chastity is its own
punishment!

Down with gravity!

All this beer will be
the urination of me

The Hernia Society
needs your support

Trifles and Tangents

Imagine the Headlines!

Lovers in the midst of an affair hold two things most dear: opportunity and discretion. That's why Dr. Brian Richards of Kent was drawn so reluctantly to the tiny sports car in Regent's Park, London, on a July evening in 1976. But the constantly blaring horn signaled emergency and he was, after all, a doctor.

In the cramped back seat, a couple was immobilized in a loving but painful embrace. The gentleman had slipped a disc in mid-writhe and could not be moved. The fire department had to cut away the back of the car so that the pair could be lifted out and disentangled under Dr. Richards' professional direction.

As the gentleman was sped off to hospital, his lover, semi-clad and totally shocked, wondered aloud to the crowd that had gathered how she was going to explain the car's condition to her husband.

Imagine what the tabloids did with that one! Or even what they would have done to the likes of poor Romeo and Juliet!

See if you can match the lovers with these tabloid "come-ons."

1. __________ Defies Her Father To Meet __________ In Family Crypt.

2. Fanatical Jealousy Drives __________ To Smother __________ As Domestic Tiff Gets Out Of Hand.

3. __________ Regains __________ After Secret Deal In Hades But Loses Her Again.

4. How Well Can __________ Swim? Reliable Source Says He Crosses Hellespont Nightly To Meet __________.

5. What Were __________ And __________ Doing In The Park When The Lions Were Loose?

6. Will The Monastery Keep __________ From __________? "We'll See To It" Says Prioress.

7. King Mark Cheated By Love Potion Death Pact Of __________ And __________.

8. Why Did __________ Hire A Notorious Unlicensed Barber? Does __________ Know?

9. Agent Denies That __________ Prays Nightly To Statue Of __________.

10. Who Is Looking After Rome While __________ Dallies With __________?

a. Thisbe	*k.* Delilah
b. Antony	*l.* Romeo
c. Heloise	*m.* Othello
d. Leander	*n.* Pyramus
e. Tristram	*o.* Hero
f. Abelard	*p.* Pygmalion
g. Cleopatra	*q.* Galatea
h. Samson	*r.* Isolde
i. Desdemona	*s.* Juliet
j. Orpheus	*t.* Eurydice

Contemplator's Corner

1. The first thing Geoff Dilley heard when he stepped down off the train in London was someone calling his name. It was a friend he had not seen in years.

   "Geoff! What a coincidence! How wonderful to see you! It's been—what—ten years? Do you know that I'm married now? This is my daughter."

   A little girl made a few very shy steps toward Geoff.

   "Hi there," Geoff said to the little girl. "What's your name?"

   "I've got the same name my mother has," the little girl answered.

   "Ah, then you're Maria," said Geoff.

   How did he know?

2. Beau got on a train at Halifax, headed for Boston. It is a six-hour trip with one half-hour stop. Two hours later Rufus got on a train at Boston headed for Halifax. This train travels at an average speed exactly double that of the one coming from Halifax, but it makes two half-hour stops. The two trains use the same line.

   When they meet, who will be closer to Halifax, Beau or Rufus?

3. Mrs. Mervyn Millstone gave birth to Mary and Marty Millstone between 2300 hours and 2315 hours on July 31, 1964. Yet Mary and Marty are not twins.

   How is this possible?

visuthink

1. This one is just a review. You probably learned it in the fourth grade or so, and then used it to get through dull classes for years afterward.

The task is to trace this envelope, without ever taking your finger off the paper, without retracing a line, and without ever crossing a line.

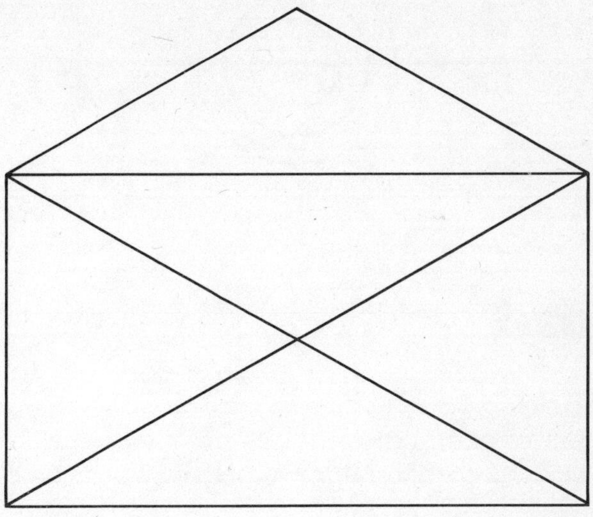

2. If memory served you, then try this one. The same rules apply: no retracing, no crossing, and don't take your finger off the paper.

3. If you're really good, this should pose no problems. Same rules!

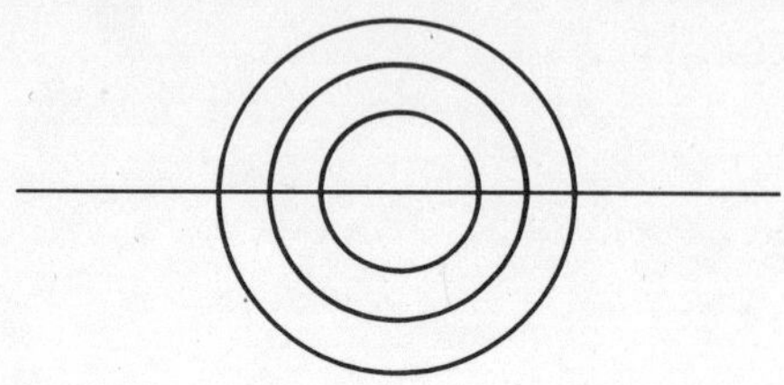

In a Word

Letter Slide

In each of the boxes below, there are five words, each five letters long. In each of the boxes, the five words all begin with the identical letter.

Your task is to find the five words in each box. You must use every letter, and a letter is used only once.

The letters used to form each five-letter word are always adjacent, either above, below, beside, or diagonal to the letter used previously.

We have done one for you

1.

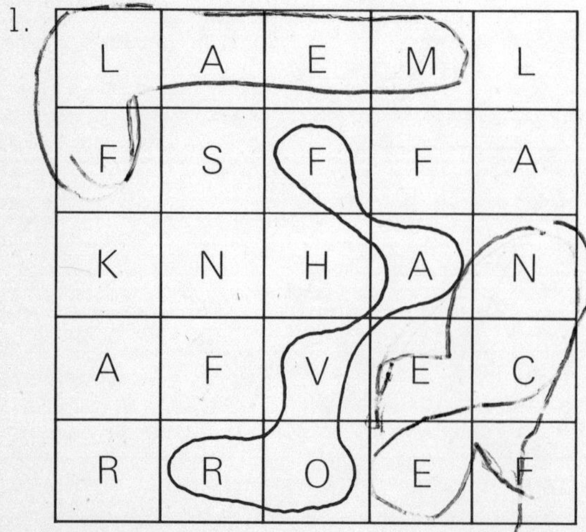

L	A	E	M	L
F	S	F	F	A
K	N	H	A	N
A	F	V	E	C
R	R	O	E	F

2.

P	E	W	A	R
R	O	P	E	P
M	E	F	O	U
I	P	O	R	P
R	P	R	E	S

3.

T	C	R	M	E
I	E	A	T	P
T	D	H	Y	T
E	C	A	T	A
E	X	X	E	R

Trifles and Tangents

Along the World's Longest Unguarded Border

Maybe the reason that the longest unguarded border in the world is just that—*unguarded*—is because it's so hard for Canadians and Americans to organize a fight.

Take the War of 1812 for instance. When a British courier from York burst into the officer's mess at Fort George on June 28, 1812, to announce the declaration of war, he was embarrassed to find American officers from Fort Niagara up the river. They were guests for dinner. Both sides agreed it would be in bad taste to start fighting right away, so they finished dinner and agreed to withhold hostilities at least until the Americans were officially informed too. There was quite a wait, since Washington had chosen to inform the Niagara frontier by mail.

1. What Canadian provinces border on the Great Lakes?

2. What four American states start with the letter "I"?

3. What two American states border on the largest number of other states?

4. What three Canadian provinces have borders with only one other province?

5. How many states were part of the United States in 1947?

6. How many provinces were part of Canada in 1947?

7. How many Canadian provinces have entirely straight-line borders? (one or two?)

8. How many U.S. states have entirely straight-line borders? (four, or six or nine?)

9. How many U.S. states can you name whose land mass touches the border with Canada along the 49th parallel?

10. How many Canadian provinces do not physically touch the border with the United States?

11. How many U.S. states and Canadian provinces together end with the letter "A"?

12. Which Canadian province was named after a British princess? And which U.S. state after a British king?

13. How many Canadian provinces and American states together have "New" in their name?

14. Omitting the Yukon and Northwest Territories and District of Columbia, which three of the sixty states and provinces have the longest names?

IN A WORD

Letter Barter

Exchange two letters in each pair of words below, one from each word, and you will produce pairs of words that are closely related.

For example, in the pair

LEAVES and BROAD,

by exchanging the E in LEAVES with the O in BROAD, you will produce

LOAVES and BREAD.

No other letters move, in either word.

1.	TAP	CHARM
2.	WANDER	OWE
3.	SPINE	WIGS
4.	WATER	BEG
5.	SCORN	TWEETY
6.	SHOP	TINDER
7.	CAR	DEFAME
8.	STRING	FORM
9.	SAG	BACK
10.	QUILT	STILE

visuthink

1. You don't need a pencil for this one, but if you want to—go ahead! Probably a pencil would make it easier.

   The task is to stroke out (or otherwise eliminate) dots from this diagram so that there are only *four* dots left in each row, and four in each column. However, the maximum number you may stroke out is *six*.

●	●	●	●	●
●	●	●	●	●
●	●	●	●	●
●	●	●	●	●
●	●	●	●	●

2. For this one you probably need a pencil. So if you're using someone else's book, don't press too hard. (Or buy your own book and press as hard as you want!)

The task is to add *six* more dots to the diagram so that there are *three*, no more no less, in each row *and* column.

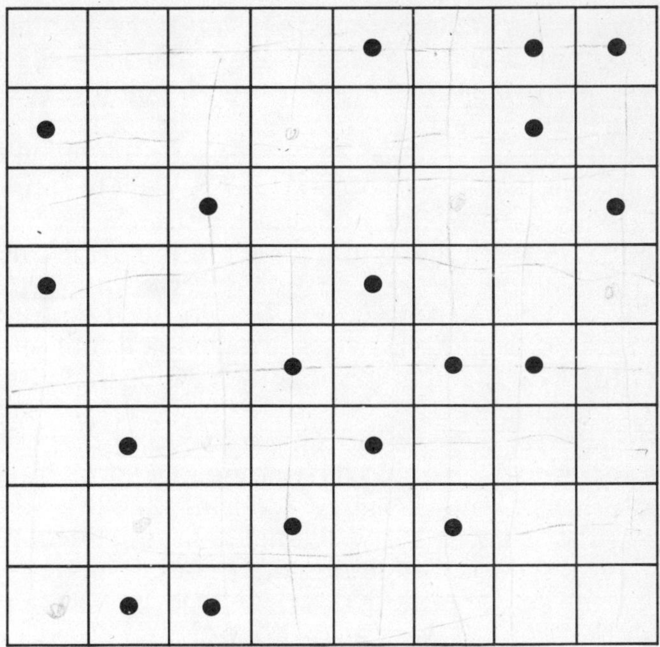

Diverting Articles

And You Think You Bought a Lemon?

James Dean, Hollywood actor and all-round rebel of the silver-screen set in the early 1950s, died in his car in California, on September 30, 1955. Archduke Franz Ferdinand of Austria-Hungary died in his car, at Sarajevo, Yugoslavia, on June 28, 1914. Beyond this, it would seem, neither man had anything whatever in common with the other. The archduke was shot by an assassin; Dean was driving at breakneck speed when a car made a left turn in front of him. Dean was twenty-four years old, a bachelor, and a commoner; Franz Ferdinand was fifty-one, of royal blood, and his wife died with him in their car. They lived in different countries, at different times, and neither man would even have been able to imagine what life was like for the other. Nothing, absolutely nothing in common—except for their cars. Ferdinand died in a bright red custom-made phaeton, an open touring car built especially for his use in Sarajevo. James Dean died in a silver-gray 1955 Porsche Spyder. And there was something very strange about both cars.

Everyone but the owners felt strange premonitions about these cars. The Duchess Sophie did not want to get into the phaeton that June day for her first—and last—ride. She insisted there was something about the car that frightened her. Dean's colleagues were reluctant to ride with him. Alec Guiness urged him to get rid of it. Ursula Andress told him it gave her a bad feeling. However, it was not until after both men met their deaths that it became obvious that these cars were strange indeed.

George Barris, a car designer, bought the wrecked Porsche for its parts. He sold the engine to a hobby racer, Dr. Troy McHenry of Beverly Hills, California, and the drive train to another hobby racer, Dr. William Eschrid of Burbank. Both doctors had the parts installed in their cars. In their very first races, Eschrid's car rolled over, and he was seriously injured; McHenry's car went out of control, and he was killed.

A third racing car buff bought the Porsche's two front tires. Weeks later on a California highway both blew out simultaneously. By this time Barris refused to sell any more parts and instead gave the rest of the car to the California Highway Patrol who planned to use it as a safety exhibit. It was taken to Fresno and stored in a garage. That night, the garage and every vehicle in it—except the Porsche—was destroyed by fire. The Porsche had a slightly scorched right rear fender.

Some weeks later, George Barkuis, a state employee, was towing the wreck to Salinas. En route, his truck went out of control; Barkuis was thrown out of the cab; the wreck came loose, fell down on top of him and crushed him.

In 1956 the car was on display at a high school in Sacramento when it suddenly fell off its pedestal, breaking a student's hip. Not long after, it was being transported along a freeway near Oakland when it suddenly broke in two, fell onto the road and caused an accident. In 1959, while on review in New Orleans, it suddenly broke into eleven distinct pieces.

Even the final end of the Porsche is mysterious. In 1960 it was on display in Miami. After the display, it was put on a truck bound for Los Angeles. On the way, the truck, the Porsche and the driver went missing. No one has ever been able to trace them.

The Archduke's car was involved in an equally strange series of incidents that led many to believe that, like James Dean's Porsche, it was cursed.

The assassination of Franz Ferdinand was the spark that started World War I. A week after the war began, General Potiorek of the Fifth Austrian Corps seized the governor's house at Sarajevo. With it came the car. Twenty-one days later Potiorek botched a major battle at Valievo, where he later died insane, in a poorhouse.

The car was taken over by a captain on his staff. Nine days later this captain struck two Croatian peasants with the car, killed them and then swerved into a tree. His body had to be pried from the wreckage.

The wreckage was ignored for five years until, in 1919, the new governor of Yugoslavia ordered the car repaired for his own use. Within four months, he had four accidents, and in one of them lost his right arm. The governor ordered the car destroyed, but a Doctor Srkis asked to buy it. Six months later he was found dead, pinned underneath it on a back country road. The car had rolled over him. It was only dented.

The doctor's widow sold the car to a jeweler, who committed suicide. The next owner was another doctor, whose patients wouldn't come near him because of what they presumed to be a curse. So he sold it to a racing driver in Switzerland who promptly smashed it against a stone wall. He was killed instantly.

Back to Sarajevo it went, this time to a wealthy farmer. One morning it stalled on the road, and the farmer convinced a passing teamster to use his horses to tow it into the city. The team had not gone very far when the car roared into power, knocked the horses into an open ditch, and rolled over on a curve. The farmer lived only a few hours.

Its final owner was a garage mechanic, Tiber Hirshfeld, who repaired it, painted it blue, and then, on the way to a wedding, drove it into a concrete bridge. Hirshfeld and four passengers were killed instantly. After Hirshfeld, no one would touch the car. In fact, although it presumably sits today in a museum in Vienna, there are those who claim that this is only a replica, and that the real car, like Dean's, has disappeared.

Without question, the strange story of this car and of Dean's Porsche is owing at least in part to coincidence. But the line between the explainable and the unexplainable is a fine one, and the temptation to believe that mysterious forces were involved with these two cars is strong indeed.

Trifles and Tangents

True? Or False?

It's interesting to reflect that Buddha's name was not Buddha. It was Siddhartha Gautama. Buddha really should be *The* Buddha. It is a title meaning "Enlightened One." For that matter, Siddhartha Gautama was not Chinese either. He was Indian.

Armed with this knowledge, you should be able to separate truth from conjecture in the following items.

True, or false?

1. Queen Victoria's mother tongue was not English.
2. There were no human survivors at the Battle of the Little Big Horn.
3. Alfred Lord Tennyson wrote *The Charge of the Heavy Brigade*.
4. The Douglas fir tree is not a fir tree.
5. The singular of scampi is scampus.
6. The first name of Miss Brooks on the "Our Miss Brooks" radio show was Eve.
7. King George VI of England was not really named George.

8. Pittsburgh, Pennsylvania, is named after British Prime Minister William Pitt.
9. *Time*'s Man of the Year in 1942 was Josef Stalin.
10. The second most popular surname in North America is *Johnson*.
11. Dieter Klaus Volt, a pioneer in electricity, is credited with the discovery of electrical current.
12. Gustave Eiffel was one of the contributing designers of the Statue of Liberty.
13. Brigham Young was the first to open a department store.
14. Among Anna Edson Taylor's major lifetime accomplishments was being the first person to go over Niagara Falls in a barrel.

ICE-BREAKERS

Questions They Can't Possibly Answer

What's the biggest role Shakespeare ever wrote?
(Falstaff. 1,178 lines in the two *Henry IV* plays and 436 lines in *The Merry Wives of Windsor*, giving him 1,614, or 192 more lines than Hamlet who is in second place.)

If you fold a piece of paper in half, four times, how many creases do you get?
(15)

How long is "quick as a wink"?
(About 1/10 of a second.)

From what animal do we get catgut?
(Sheep)

Has a pope ever been murdered?
(Yes. Twenty-six of them!)

What did Wyatt Earp and Casanova have in common?
(They were both professional faro dealers, besides the fact that both at various points in their lives were lawmen *and* law breakers.)

Name two words in the English language that contain the vowels A, E, I, O, U, in order.
(Abstemious and facetious. They are the only two.)

At what age does a filly become a mare?
(Five years)

What has been the most frequent first name for royalty in Europe since the fall of the Roman Empire?
(Probably Charles. There have been around 75, but whether some of them could be called kings is disputable. The same controversy applies to Henry's, James', and Louis's, although these are clearly fewer in number.)

What is Jim Blane's secret?
(He is the only person besides Tonto who knows the Lone Ranger's true identity.)

What is the shortest verse in the bible?
("Jesus wept." John 11:35)

What does "Tarzan" mean in ape language?
(It means "white skin.")

IN A WORD

Tumbleword

1. The object of Tumbleword is to make one *three*-letter word from the letters in the top line of the diagram.

2. Then enter that three-letter word into the empty squares in the line immediately below.

3. Rearrange the remaining six letters in the first line to make a six-letter word, and enter it at the bottom.

4. Repeat the procedure for each successive line until you reach the bottom line, where there will be six remaining letters. Rearrange these to form a six-letter word.

For a perfect score you must use all sixty letters in the diagram, and make ten six-letter words. Plurals and words beginning with capital letters are not allowed.

Hint: To guarantee a perfect score, none of the letters of each three-letter word should be used again for the next three-letter word.

To start you off, the three-letter word in the first line is PLY.

N	N	P	T	O	L	A	Y	C	
R	E	R				T	A	A	
B	M	S				L	U	V	
R	C	E				M	I	E	
T	L	R				R	A	D	
F	R	E				Z	L	U	
P	N	L				I	R	O	
O	O	R				E	E	C	
G	T	D				I	V	C	
B	■		R	■			■	E	

Contemplator's Corner

We can't publish a book like this one without including the following puzzle. It's one of the all-time greats. When you solve it, you join a company that goes back to at least pre-Hittite times. When you've done it, put your mind to the scholarship one that follows it.

1. When Dr. Muddle broke out of the jungle to the river's edge, the army of ants was close behind. He had only a little time to get himself and his cargo across. But his inflatable rubber dinghy would hold only himself, and either his panther or his goat or the box of tin cans, not all three at once. Yet he had to get everything across without leaving the panther alone to eat the goat or the goat alone to eat the cans. How?

2. Just down the river the problem is even more perplexing. Escaping from the same army of ants are three prison guards and three prisoners. They have one two-person inflatable dinghy. Swimming is impossible. Besides, the piranha wouldn't permit it. The guards cannot permit themselves to be outnumbered on either side of the river. The prisoners, on the other hand, don't know the jungle at all, and would never attempt to escape without at least one guard to act as guide. They have to cross. How?

THE MAGIC OF NUMBERS

No doubt it has often occurred to you that the number three seems to crop up more often than any other in our lives. Why, for example, are there Three Little Pigs, Three Wishes, or Three Trials? Why is Cinderella the youngest of three sisters and why didn't Goldilocks have to deal with four bears? Why are there Three Musketeers (Athos, Porthos, and Aramis), Three Little Maids (Yum-Yum, Peep-Bo, Pitti-Sing) and Three Stooges? There are Three Wise Men, Three R's, even Three Men in a Tub.

It's no accident that the number three appears so often. Three is the number of mystery. Even a famous work such as Dante's *Divine Comedy* recognizes that numbers have a special meaning. The poem has three parts of thirty-three cantos each and has three main characters. Like many scholars of his time, Dante was aware of the secret meaning of numbers. He was a student of the ancient science of numerology.

Numerology is the study of the occult importance of numbers. Dante and the writers of fairy tales often used the number three because it can represent time (past, present and future) as well as space (length, width and thickness). Three also seems to fit nicely with the natural rhythm of activities like reading. Notice how many times a writer uses three examples, in magazines particularly.

Some people believe that numerology can be used to foretell the future or to uncover answers to the mysteries of life. Devil worshipers, for instance, use numbers in their ceremonies. Perhaps because the number two sometimes signifies the devil in opposition to God, the instruments, vestments and ornaments used in black magic rites are always in twos. And witches always make certain that covens have thirteen members.

Some numbers, especially seven, are thought to be very special. There are seven sacraments, seven deadly sins, seven wonders of the world, seven seas, seven days of the week, and seven years of bad luck for breaking a mirror. The seventh son of a seventh son (or daughter) is said to have supernatural powers.

The number 100 also has a nice ring to it. Kids count to 100; it's often a savings plateau for money. Sleeping Beauty was "out" for 100 years. John Scopes' fine in the famous Monkey Trial in Dayton, Tennessee, in 1925 was $100.

Other numbers, like nine for example, are used by stage magicians and by pseudo-psychics. Here is one trick that you can learn easily. Give someone the following instructions:

- Write down a four-digit number; *cover it so that I can't see it*!
- Beneath it, write another four-digit number that I can see.
- Now, I'll give you a four-digit number.
- Now, you write a four-digit number.

- I'll give you another one now.
- Add the whole column, including the number you kept covered. Hide your answer but let me see the whole column and I'll add it in two seconds!

The trick is that each of the two numbers you give yourself, if added to the number right above it, must total 9,999. If you do this both times, the sum will always be 20,000 plus the first number, which your friend kept hidden, minus 2.

Example:

4,682	(hidden by friend)
2,718	– friend
7,281	– you
5,271	– friend
4,728	– you
24,680	(20,000 + 4,682 – 2)

It is generally believed that numerology began with Pythagoras, a Greek philosopher of the sixth century BC. He felt that certain patterns of numbers explained the workings of the universe.

And in many ways the belief holds water too. Here, for example, is a mildly complicated but fascinating technique for discovering on what day of the week you were born, on what day Christmas will fall in 1998, or what day of the week was VE day (May 8, 1945).

The first thing you need is a key number for each month, as follows:

April, July	=0
Jan., Oct.	=1
May	=2
Aug.	=3
Feb., March, Nov.	=4
June	=5
Sept., Dec.	=6

Now use this procedure. (Try May 8, 1945.)

Step One
Take the last two digits of the year (45) and add one-quarter of that number. (When the number is not divisible by 4, drop to the next *lowest* number that is. In this case it is 44, so that the one-quarter to be added is 11 (44 ÷ 11 = 11).
Therefore Step One is 45 + 11 = 56

Step Two
Add the key number for the month. (May is 2.)
56 + 2 = 58

Step Three
Add the day of the month.
58 + 8 = 62

Step Four
Divide by 7. It's the remainder that's important. 66 ÷ 7 = 9 with a remainder of 3.

Step Five
Now apply one more code. The remainder you will have will give you the day of the week, as follows:

Sunday = 1
Monday = 2
Tuesday = 3
Wednesday = 4
Thursday = 5
Friday = 6
Saturday = 0

Therefore VE day was a Tuesday!

There are a few trivial adjustments. (We said it was *mildly* complicated, didn't we?) For dates in the 1800s add 2 to the remainder in Step Four. For the 2000s go back one day.

Also, for January and February dates in leap years go back one day. (Nothing is perfect!)

Finally, any trivia freak knows that this is applicable only to Gregorian calendar dates, and not Julian. That's what's so fascinating about numbers. You can cover almost any exception you want and most people will accept it. Numbers, you see, are mysterious.

Answers

Page 1, Trifles and Tangents

1. James Meredith was the first black student to register at the University of Mississippi, in October 1962.

2. Margaret Sinclair is the maiden name of Margaret Trudeau.

3. James W. McCord was one of the Watergate break-in crew.

4. Bessie Wallis Warfield was the famous American divorcée who became the Duchess of Windsor in 1938.

5. Edward Brooke was the first black person to be elected to the U.S. Senate (1966).

6. Clifford Irving wrote the famous "non"-biography of Howard Hughes.

7. Richard Starkey is Ringo Starr's real name.

8. Dr. Allan Dafoe delivered the Dionne quintuplets on May 28, 1934.

9. Amanda Blake starred as Miss Kitty on *Gunsmoke*.

10. Valentina Tereshkova was the first woman astronaut to circle the globe (1963).

11. Francis Chichester sailed single-handed around the world.

12. Florence Chadwick was the first woman to swim the English Channel both ways.

13. Martha Mitchell was the wife of Attorney-General John Mitchell in the Nixon presidency and became famous for her telephone calls to the press.

14. James Cross was British trade commissioner to Canada and in 1970 was kidnapped by the FLQ, a Quebec separatist organization. Five days later they captured and murdered Pierre Laporte, Quebec's minister of labor, bringing about one of Canada's worst domestic crises.

15. Bill Barilko scored the winning goal in overtime to win the Stanley Cup for the Toronto Maple Leafs in 1951. He disappeared in a light plane in northern Canada shortly after.

16. Felix Leiter was (is?) James Bond's CIA contact.

17. When Algeria finally became an independent country in 1962, Ferhat Abbas was its first president.

18. Leader of the unsuccessful Biafran secessionists in the Nigerian Civil War, 1967–69. During this war, television showed for the first time some of the worst examples of mass starvation the Western World has ever seen. Ojukwu was a readily available interview subject.

Page 1, Visuthink

1. what goes up must come down
   mixed company
   spots before the eyes
   pie in the sky
   it's against the law

2. reading between the lines
   round of applause
   one in a million
   calculated risk
   $e = mc^2$

3. half mine half yours
   Noel
   scatterbrained
   white lies
   bad spell of weather

Page 2, Sherlock of the John

Miles would not have seen that the eyes were blue if the phony policeman was wearing sunglasses.

Page 4, Contemplator's Corner

1. $545 + 5 = 550$

2. A dozen, a gross, and a score,
   Plus three times the square root of four,
   If divided by seven,
   Plus five times eleven,
   Yields nine squared and not a bit more.

3. The match. What else!

4. 72. The rest are 10^2, 6^2, 4^2, 2^2

Page 5, In a Word

1.	rivet	2.	fender
	anvil		bundle
	cover		hinder
	hovel		candle
	liver		random
	havoc		sandal
	savor		bandit
	coven		vendor

Page 6, Trifles and Tangents

1. billiards, bowling, golf, bocce, cricket, handball, lacrosse, croquet, polo, field hockey, baseball; there are others

2. golf

3. horseshoe pitching

4. 25. The home team hits a home run on the first pitch, making the score 1–0. Thereafter there are 3 pitches per inning, including the first inning, but excluding the ninth. $3 \times 8 = 24 + 1$ for the homer = 25.

5. 1948

6. It was the first World Series. It was also a nine game series. Boston took it 5 games to 3. There were nine game series in 1919, '20, '21 as well.

7. Robert Fitzsimmons, 1897–99 (Australian)
   Tommy Burns, 1906–1908 (Canadian; real name Noah Brusso)
   Max Schmeling, 1930–32 (German)
   Primo Carnera, 1933–34 (Italian)
   Ingemar Johansson 1959–60 (Swedish)

8. December 19, 1917

9. Barbara Ann Scott in 1948. If Donald Jackson and Otto and Maria Jelinek sprang to mind, they won world championship titles in 1962 but not Olympic golds. Barbara Ann Scott, for what it's worth, won world championships too in 1947 *and* 1948.

10. Cindy Nicholas

11. The Gordon International Medal Series between Canada and the United States was first held at Montreal in 1884. The Strathcona Cup between Canada and Scotland was first held in 1903.

12. All three are for golf series between Britain and the United States. The Ryder is for professionals. The other two are for amateurs.

13. *a.* tiddleywinks
    b. billiards
    c. weight-lifting
    d. jai-lai
    e. archery

Page 8, Contemplator's Corner

1. Jack Atkin and the geraniums are on the north. If Ron Minaker is directly opposite with the chrysanthemums, then he can be directly left of Ron Forrester's greenhouse. Bill Lacroix will be opposite Ron Forrester, but since Lacroix does not grow poinsettias, they must be Forrester's. Lacroix has the Easter lilies.

2. The first move is #4 stick left, to T with #1. The second is #7 left to T with #3. If you can't finish from here, then you should not be doing this problem!

Page 9, Visuthink

1. (E). The horizontal line changes to vertical. The figure on the right of the line changes to black. The figure on the left is unchanged, but moves to the other side.

2. J is the odd one out.

Page 10, Trifles and Tangents

1. They were all top singles (for the years 1956, 1962, 1957 and 1951 respectively).

2. Cowboy singer Gene Autry. The radio show was "Melody Ranch."

3. Guy Lombardo and His Royal Canadians.

4. No, not "Rock Around the Clock," but a song called "Crazy Man Crazy."

5. *a.* "While you've a Lucifer to light your fag"—Felix Powell, British army sergeant, won a World War I competition for this song. The idea was to write a morale building song for the troops. (Powell died by his own hand in 1942.)

b. "You may search everywhere, but none can compare"—from a Broadway musical of 1898.

c. "We hurry to my blue heaven"—theme song of Gene Austin.

d. "If you got the money honey, I got the time"—made popular by Hank Williams.

e. "Would you stand up and walk out on me?"—from "A Little Help From My Friends," the Beatles.

6. Nova Scotian, Hank Snow. He had at least one best-seller on the charts from 1949–1970.

7. *a.* "Wait 'Till the Sun Shines, Nellie"
   b. "Sweet Adeline"
   c. "Let Me Call You Sweetheart"
   d. "My Gal Sal"
   e. "Meet Me Tonight in Dreamland"

Page 11, In a Word

1. pie shell
2. Odd Fellows
3. vast emptiness
4. Evelyn Waugh
5. running free
6. tying run
7. Yaqui Indians
8. Middle East
9. anti-nuclear
10. kewpie doll
11. even steven

The saying is "Poverty makes few friends."

Page 12, Contemplator's Corner

1. five
2. Turn the page upside down.
3. True. $9 \div 9 + 99 = 100$
4. All of them!

Page 12, Sherlock of the John

If the young man had stood in the heat for almost an hour, he would not have been able to break off a piece of chocolate bar that had been in his shirt pocket.

Page 13, Trifles and Tangents

1. Arion
2. (b); (b)
3. (c)
4.

Autry	Champion*
Wellington	Copenhagen
Cid	Babieca
Cody	Brigham
Google	Spark Plug
Mix	Tony
Mix's first	Old Blue
Cassidy	Topper
Alexander the Great	Bucephalus
Dudley Do-Right	Horse

*There were three Champions. The first was Tom Mix's Tony Jr.

5. Mexico in 1968 (Tom Gayford, Jim Elder, Jim Day)
6. Generally polo is played four a side, especially on the large outdoor field. But if it is played inside on a smaller field, three a side is the norm.
7. *a.* The Plate and the Derby are both 1¼ miles. The Preakness is 1 3/16 miles; the Belmont, 1½. The Queen's Plate was first run in 1859 when the distance was 1⅛ miles. It changed in 1956. The Derby began later, in 1875. It was 1½ miles until 1896. The Preakness began in 1873 and the Belmont even earlier in 1867, but the Queen's Plate is the oldest.
   b. Ron Turcotte of Grand Falls, New Brunswick, rode Secretariat in 1:59.2, only 3/5ths of a second faster than Northern Dancer in 1964 (ridden by Bill Hartack, an American).

Page 19, Contemplator's Corner

1.

P	V	O
O	P	V
V	O	P

2. Enter 1 to 5 in order in the top row; then always enter the next row down, beginning with the middle number of the row above.

3.

<table>
<tr><td></td><td>4</td><td>6</td><td></td></tr>
<tr><td>7</td><td>1</td><td>8</td><td>2</td></tr>
<tr><td></td><td>3</td><td>5</td><td></td></tr>
</table>

Page 20, Trifles and Tangents

1. George Jorgensen Jr., became Christine Jorgensen
2. Pheidippides
3. Johnny Wayne and Frank Shuster
4. Christine Keeler and Mandy Rice-Davies
5. Howdy Doody
6. Gildersleeve. The Great Gildersleeve
7. Esther Williams
8. Max Aiken
9. Nadia Comenici of Romania
10. William Stephenson
11. John T. Scopes
12. Alexander Dubcek

Page 23, Sherlock of the John

The drapes in the office had been closed.

Page 26, Trifles and Tangents

1. Libya
2. Panama
3. Norway
4. Nepal
5. Haiti
6. Switzerland
7. Australia
8. Romania
9. U.S.A.
10. Brazil
11. Canada

Page 27, In a Word

1. tennis
2. tender
3. kitten
4. intent
5. stench
6. whiten
7. attend
8. rotten
9. hasten
10. tenure
11. beaten
12. tenant

Page 27, Visuthink

1. 64
2. 8 corners; a cube is six-sided
3. 48 cm
4. 16-one side only
   20-two sides only
   8-three sides only
5. four

Page 30, Trifles and Tangents

1. Captain Queeg
   Captain Ahab
   Captain Smollett
   Captain Nemo
   Captain Hook (all right, we know it's really a play but. . .)
2. *The Bridge of San Luis Rey* is based on a bridge collapse in Peru in 1714.
   An American Tragedy is based on an actual New York murder case.
3. Charles Dickens
4. T.C. Haliburton
5. Sinclair Lewis
6. *a.* Major—*Animal Farm*
   b. Captain Flint—*Treasure Island*
   c. Ginger—*Black Beauty*
   d. Buck—*Call of the Wild*
   e. Paddy—*The Adventures of Paddy the Beaver*

7. *a.* H. Rider Haggard. *She* (1887); *King Solomon's Mines* (1885). The latter was his response to a challenge to write a story as adventurous as *Treasure Island*.
   b. Louisa May Alcott in 1874. It never touched *Little Women* (1868–9) or even *Little Men* (1871).
   c. James Hilton

8. *a.* Robertson Davies with the Deptford Trilogy (*Fifth Business*, 1970; *The Manticore*, 1972; *World of Wonders*, 1975).
   b. W.O. Mitchell set *Jake and the Kid* in Crocus, Saskatchewan (CBC Radio: 1949–1957; TV: 1961; pub. 1961).
   c. Faulkner wrote much of his work based on this mythical county in Mississippi.
   d. Carl Barks went to work for the Disney Studios in the 1940s and was largely responsible for Scrooge McDuck (uncle of Donald).
   e. Ingleside was one of the several places where one would find L.M. Montgomery's Anne (of Green Gables).

Page 31, Sherlock of the John

If the man has just driven up, the engine of his car will be warm. If the woman is telling the truth, her engine will be cold.

Page 34, In a Word

erie	po
volga	zambezi
platte	mersey
red	quill
yalu	potomac
caspian	aegean
xingu	rhine
swan	tiber
peace	tigris
irish	black
loire	huron
jordan	fundy
danube	elbe

Page 35, Trifles and Tangents

1. Lawrence Berra
   George Stevens
   John Henry Holliday
   Arthur Fonzarelli
   Clerow Wilson

2. Wayne King
   Ferdinand Demerara Jr.
   Eddy Arnold
   Lou Gehrig
   Betty Grable

3. They were all mules. Ruth was Festus Hagen's mount on *Gunsmoke*. Francis the Talking Mule was a movie star. Charlie O. was the mascot mule of the Oakland A's. Worthless was Dirty Sally's mule on the *Dirty Sally* TV series.

4. Kay Kayser's Kollege of Musical Knowledge

5. Rosemary's Baby

6. Floyd Patterson was the rabbit; Sonny Liston, the bear; and Joe Frazier, the turtle.

7. Graceland is the Elvis Presley mansion in Memphis, Tenn.
   Old Betsy was Davy Crockett's rifle.
   Little Boy was dropped on Hiroshima in 1945. (It was first called The Thin Man after FDR. The bomb dropped on Nagasaki *was* called The Fat Man, after Churchill.)

8. Elsie (the Borden cow)

9. Thomas Stearns Eliot
   Benjamin Franklin Goodrich
   David Herbert Lawrence
   Orenthal James Simpson

Page 39, Visuthink

1. BUDGIE

2. CAVALRY

3. WHETHER

(Each additional stroke means one more letter from the front of the alphabet, ∠ = B, △ = C, etc. Each curve means one letter from the back of the alphabet C = Z, S = Y, etc.)

Page 40, Trifles and Tangents

1. Yellow (Submarine) and Blue (Boy) would make green.

2. Yellow

3. The Purple Onion

4. Little Beaver said it to Red Ryder.

5. It is a diamond owned by Princess Dala.

6. Roy Brown

7. NL —Cincinnati Reds
   AL —Toronto Blue Jays
   —Boston Red Sox
   —Chicago White Sox
   NHL —Chicago Black Hawks
   —Detroit Red Wings
   —St. Louis Blues
   CFL —Winnipeg Blue Bombers
   NFL —Cleveland Browns
   —Green Bay Packers
   —Washington Redskins
   NASL —Vancouver Whitecaps
   NBA —Golden State Warriors
   (13 teams out of 121 teams!)

8. "The Ballad of the Green Berets"

9. Whitehall

10. "There'll Be Bluebirds Over the White Cliffs of Dover"

11. House of Lancaster—red
    House of York—white

12. *a. The Cherry Orchard*
    b. The Scarlet Letter
    c. The Red Pony
    d. The Silver Chalice
    e. Forever Amber

*The word was "tequila."

Page 45, Sherlock of the John

On farms, pioneer farms especially, the manure pile was always on the south, or southeast side of the barn, so the manure would freeze more slowly in fall and thaw more quickly in spring. At sunset, the pile would have been in shadow, and Brunt could not have had the sun in his eyes. (This one is tricky, we'll grant you.)

Page 47, Trifles and Tangents

1. *a.* Agincourt
   b. Austerlitz
   c. Lepanto
   d. Isandhlwana
   e. Marathon
   f. Tannenburg
   g. Philippi

2. *a.* Battle of Trafalgar, October 21, 1805 in Strait of Gibraltar.
   b. The Charge of the Light Brigade, 1854, led by Cardigan against the wishes of the High Command.
   c. War of 1812. Actually he said "Blow her up! Sink her! Don't give up the ship." The first part has been conveniently forgotten, especially since his sailors *did* give up the ship.
   d. "Merde!"

3. *a.* Nguyen Vo Giap, who was also the mastermind of Dien Bien Phu.
   b. General Sir Douglas Haig and Field Marshal Joseph Joffre.
   c. General Jeffrey Amherst (later Baron). Incidentally, in Benjamin West's famous painting of the death of Wolfe, almost none of the people in the painting were actually present. West offered people a spot in the painting—for a fee.
   d. Attila the Hun (406?–453)

Page 49, Visuthink

1. There are 87 triangles.
2. There are 653 triangles. The figure is produced with 33 straight lines.

Page 67, Trifles and Tangents

Rulers of England
Edward IV (1461–1470)
Stephen I (1135–1154)
William IV (1830–1837)
Richard III (1483–1485)
The last James was James II who reigned from 1685–1688.

Emperors of Rome
Marcus Aurelius (161–180)
Philip the Arab (244–249)
Diocletian (284–305)
Domitian (81–96)
Publius Vergilius Maro was a poet, author of the *Aeneid* (70–19, BC).

Presidents of the United States
James Buchanan (1857–1861)
Rutherford Hayes (1877–1881)
Chester Arthur (1881–1885)
Franklin Pierce (1853–1857)
Asher Benjamin (1773–1845) was an American architect.

Secretaries-General of the United Nations
Dag Hammarskjöld (1953–1961)
U Thant (1961–1971)
Kurt Waldheim (1971–1982)
Trygve Lie (1945–1953)

Lester Pearson was prime minister of Canada (1963–1968).

Rulers of France
Louis XVIII (1815–1824)
Henry IV (1610–1643)
Charles X (1824–1830)
Napoleon III (1848–1870)

The last Philip was Philip VI (1328–1350).

Prime Ministers of Canada
John Sparrow Thompson (1892–1894)
Charles Tupper (1896)
John Joseph Abbott (1891–1892)
Mackenzie Bowell (1894–1896)

Charles Gladstone (1877–1947) was a famous Haida carver.

Premiers of the USSR
Georgi Malenkov (1953–1955)
Nikolai Bulganin (1955–1958)
Aleksei Kosygin (1964–1977)
Nikita Kruschev (1958–1964)

Trotsky was an associate of Lenin but never held the premiership.

English Monarchies
House of Plantagenet (Henry II (1115) to Richard II (1399))
House of Lancaster (Henry IV (1399) to Henry VI (1461))
House of Hanover (George I (1714) to Victoria (1901))
House of York (Edward IV (1461) to Richard III (1483))

House of Saxony (there was a house of Saxony in Europe)

Triple Crown Winners
Sir Barton was the first to win (1919). Assault took the crown in 1946, and the famous Citation in 1948. Seattle Slew won in 1977.

Northern Dancer won the Derby and the Preakness in 1964 but then lost the Belmont Stakes to Quadrangle.

Page 70, In a Word

A		*B*	
VIVID	— DINGY	TEASE	— QUIET
BRIGHT	— CLOUDY	PESTER	— SOOTHE

C			*D*		
BLAME	—	CHEER	SCANT	—	AMPLE
REBUKE	—	PRAISE	SPARSE	—	PLENTY

E			*F*		
ROUGH	—	SLEEK	YIELD	—	FORCE
COARSE	—	SMOOTH	PERMIT	—	COMPEL

Page 73, Trifles and Tangents

1. Satchel Paige: possibly the greatest pitcher of all time. First black pitcher in majors (Cleveland Indians in 1948 at age of *42*). First game was a shut out. At 59, in 1965, he pitched two no-hit innings for K.C. Royals. Threw 50 no-hitters in the National Negro League.
2. Jackie Gleason as Ralph Kramden in *The Honeymooners*.
3. Sergeant Preston in *Challenge of the Yukon*. The dog's name was Yukon King (a dog, but raised by a wolf named Three Toes).
4. Rhett Butler in *Gone With The Wind*, played by Clark Gable.
5. *a.* Rodney Dangerfield
   b. Jack Benny
   c. Jack Parr
6. *a.* Sherwin-Williams paint
   b. Wrigley's gum
   c. Kleenex
   d. Buick
7. *a.* Parker
   b. Kaufman
   c. Rossini

Page 78, Visuthink

1. You're right. This many.

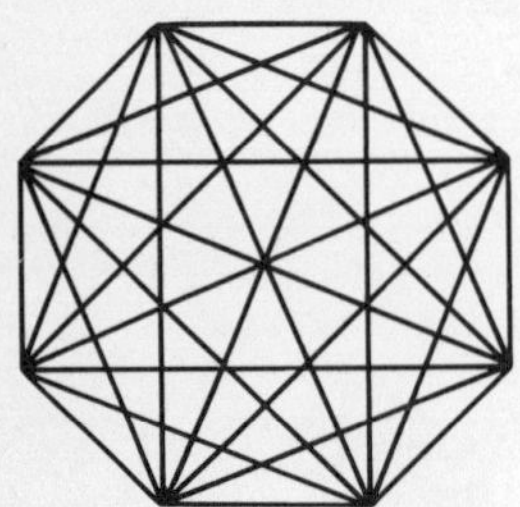

2. A, C, D, and E are incorrect.

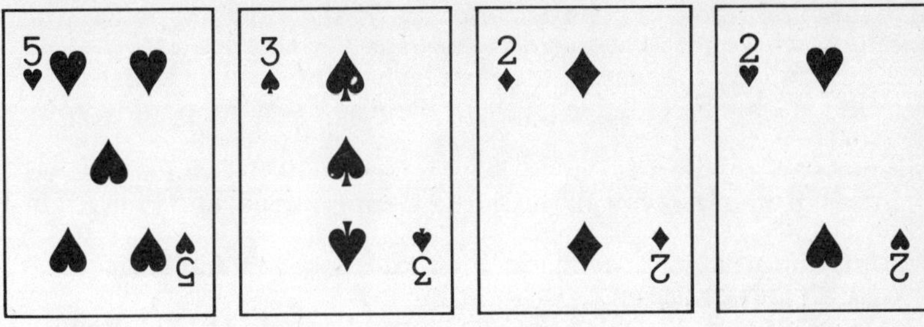

Page 80, Trifles and Tangents

1. Johnny Cash
2. Blackbeard the pirate (d. 1718)
3. The Wild One, 1954 (also starring Lee Marvin)
4. Blackjack (This is also the name of cowboy star Allen "Rocky" Lane's horse.)
5. Cincinnati Reds. The Sox lost 5 games to 3.
6. Chop Chop (The others were Chuck, Hendrickson, Stan, and Blackhawk himself.)
7. The Green Hornet (On TV the car was a 1957 Lincoln Futura.)
8. Burt Reynolds
9. True
10. Edward, the Black Prince (1330–1376)
11. The Seven Years War (1756–1763)
12. Blackleg is a contagious, usually fatal disease of cattle, and occasionally, sheep. It is also called black quarter.

Page 81, Contemplator's Corner

1. He pulled the plug.
2. VI + IV = X
3. 21 cigarettes (16 + 4 + 1)
4. $\frac{\text{H X}}{\text{G R}}$ (they are arranged by shape)

Page 84, Sherlock of the John

Mules are the offspring of a male ass or donkey, and a female horse. Although they are generally referred to as "she," mules are a sterile hybrid. A "hinny," by the way, is the result when the mother is an ass and the father is a horse. (All this might explain some of the people you know!)

President Kennedy died at Dallas, November 22, 1963. Eva Peron died in 1952, Ernest Hemingway in 1961, Clarke Gable in 1960, and Pius XII in 1958.

Elton John, Robert Louis Stevenson, Eleanor Roosevelt and Frank Sinatra were all only children.

George I of England, Nicholas I of Russia and Leopold I of Belgium, were not called the First (I) in their lifetimes. The numbering starts only after there is a second of that name. (Victoria of England, for example, is still Victoria, and not Victoria I.)

Page 85, Trifles and Tangents

1. Smiley is not one of the Seven Dwarfs.
2. Doris is not one of the Andrews Sisters.
3. The Seattle Mariners are an American League baseball team. The others are all NHL hockey teams.
4. Rossini, Elgar, Haydn and Dittersdorf were all composers. Eugenio Pacelli became Pope Pius XII.
5. Lemuel Leaver was not part of Al Capp's "Lil Abner" comic strip.
6. Madeira is not a European river.
7. Shadrach was one of the faithful Hebrews saved from the fiery furnace (Book of Daniel) but he was not, like the other three, a son of Noah.
8. Perth is a city in Australia, not a state like the others.
9. Davis (1879–1845) was the donor, in 1900 of the Davis Cup (tennis). Stanley (1841–1908) donated the Stanley Cup in 1893 (hockey). It is the oldest professional trophy in North America.
   Grey (1851–1917) gave the Grey Cup to Canadian football in 1909.
   Nelson (1907–1975) was the Ozzie Nelson of Ozzie and Harriet.
10. Don and Phil are singers (the Everly Brothers). The other brothers were all car-makers. (Gaston and Louis Chevrolet) (Horace and John Dodge) (August and Frederick Duesenberg).
11. Martin Zarcovich shot John Dillinger (1931). (There is some doubt about whether it really was Dillinger.) Pat Garrett shot Billy the Kid (1881). Bob Ford shot Jesse James (1882). There is strong evidence too that this was a setup and James simply disappeared. John Selman shot John Wesley Hardin (1895). Henri Dunant was the founder of the International Red Cross (1864).

12. Of course it's Girolamo Fracastoro, but not because the others are published writers. He is too. The others were all ambulance drivers in World War I. Fracastoro, incidentally, is credited with coining the word "syphilis" in one of his poems, around 1530.

Page 91, In a Word

1. decide
2. deed
3. sense
4. fluff
5. retire
6. hash
7. termite
8. tartar
9. church
10. kick
11. murmur
12. onion
13. window
14. alfalfa
15. phonograph

Page 95, Trifles and Tangents

1. *a.* Handel, George Frederic (1685–1759)
   b. Bach, Karl Philipp Emanuel (1714–1788) (Johann's second son)
   c. Copeland, Aaron (b. 1900)
   d. Scriabin, Alexander Nikolaievich (1872–1915)
   e. Kreisler, Fritz (1875–1962)
   f. Sullivan, Arthur Seymour (1842–1900)
   g. Mozart, Johann George Leopold (1719–1787) (Wolfgang's father*)
   h. Rimski-Korsakov, Nikolai Andreivich (1844–1908)
   i. Brahms, Johannes (1833–1897)
   j. Mussorsky, Modest Petrovich (1835–1881)

*Wolfgang's name was: Johannes Chrysostomus Wolfgangus Theophilus Mozart. Amadeus is the Latin form of Theophilus, but it was never legally his name.

2. a. percussion b. woodwind c. brass

3. Leonard Bernstein—"West Side Story" in 1957
   Ludwig van Beethoven—"The Emperor Concerto" in 1809
   George & Ira Gershwin and D. Heyward—"Porgy and Bess" in 1935
   Sergei Rachmaninov—"Rhapsody on a Theme of Paganini" in 1934
   Benjamin Britten—"The Young Person's Guide to the Orchestra" in 1946
   Robert Wilson (an American)—"The Life and Times of Joseph Stalin" in 1973 (not frequently performed, especially since the performance time is 13 1/2 hours)

Page 96, Contemplator's Corner

1. The spare was flat.
2. Once. After that the numeral becomes 20.5.
3. Open each link on the three link piece, and use them to join the other four fragments.
4. Five

Page 97, Sherlock of the John

There is no September 31.

Page 100, Trifles and Tangents

1. *a.* 1953
   b. 1960
   c. 1821
   d. 1759
   e. 1958
   f. 1572
   g. 1501
   h. 1564
   i. 1905
   j. 1649

2. *a.* The D-Day landing of World War II
   b. Neil Armstrong steps onto the moon
   c. These dates did not exist. When the Gregorian calendar replaced the Julian on September 2, there was an 11-day gap that needed to be filled to bring the calendar into tune with the Earth's motion around the sun. Thus the pope deemed that September 2 would be followed by September 14. (There were riots!)
   d. The beginning of the world, according to Calvinist theologian Bishop James Usshur, an Irish churchman famous for his learning. This date was accepted as authoritative for several hundred years.
   e. Julius Caesar was assassinated in Rome.
   f. The failure of the bomb plot to assassinate Hitler, led by Colonel (Count) Claus von Stauffenberg. Many believed Hitler received injury to his left arm, which tended to dangle uselessly. Not so. It was the right which was wounded.

3. *a.* 1954
   b. 1610
   c. 1885 (in the Riel Rebellion at the Battle of Cut Knife Hill)
   d. 1445
   e. 1928
   f. 1498
   g. 1876
   h. 1681 (within two years either way, since the documentation is not precise)

4. *a.* Beatles last performance: Candlestick Park, San Francisco, August 29, 1966. The USS *Pueblo* was captured on January 23, 1968.
   b. Adrian II was pope from 867 to 872. (He is sometimes called Hadrian.) Eric the Red landed at Greenland in 981.
   c. Einstein published in 1905. Frank James died in 1915.
   d. Anton van Leeuwenhoek described spermatozoa in 1677. William Morton, a dentist, first used ether on a patient in 1846.

5. Father Hennepin saw Niagara in 1678. Since then, only the years 1881 and 1961 qualify.

Page 104, In a Word

1. log	8. crane
2. punch	9. down
3. racket	10. club
4. sack	11. bar
5. board	12. box
6. flag	13. match
7. scale	14. cross

Page 105, Contemplator's Corner

1. Always move each succeeding coin *to* the point from where the preceding one began. For example, if you place a coin on A and slide it to D; then place your next coin on F and slide it to A; your third on C and slide it to F, etc.

2. Twenty-three.

Page 108, Trifles and Tangents

1. s + l	6. f + c
2. m + i	7. e + r
3. j + t	8. k + h
4. d + o	9. p + q
5. n + a	10. b + g

Page 110, Contemplator's Corner

1. Geoff's friend was the mother.
2. When they *meet*, Beau and Rufus will be the same distance from Halifax.
3. Mary and Marty had a brother, Milty, born at 2307 hours, so they are triplets.

Page 110, Visuthink

1.

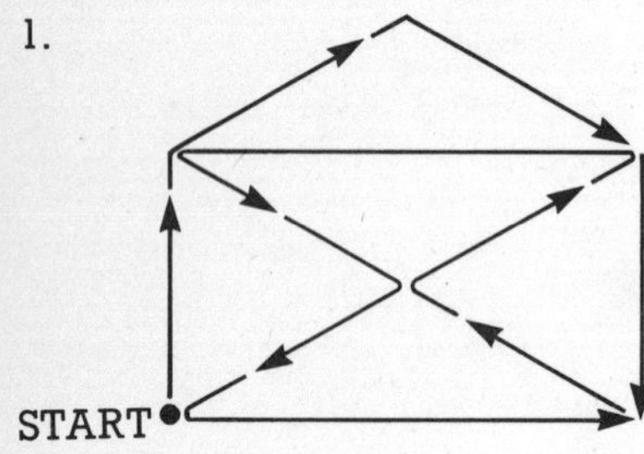

3.

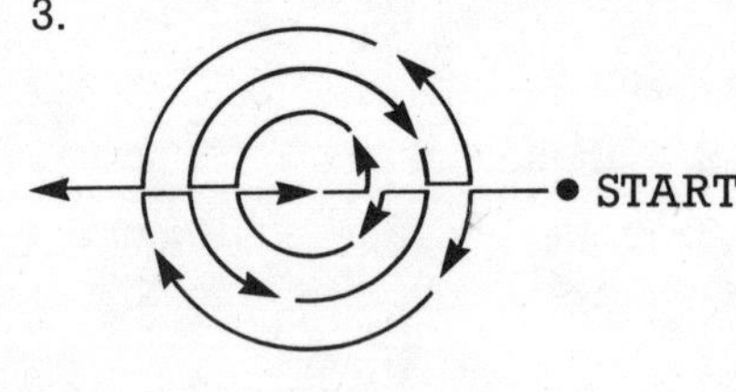

2.

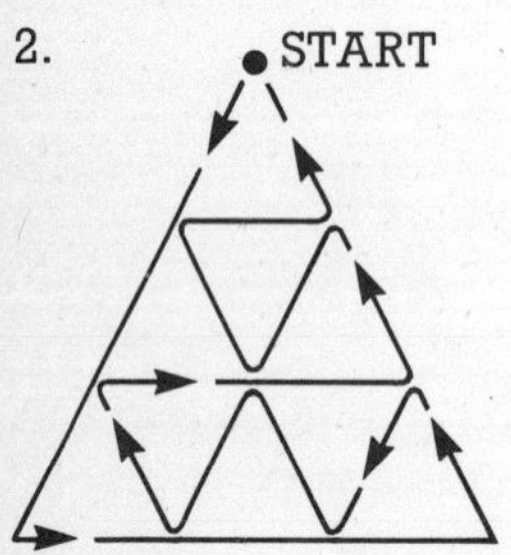

Page 112, In a Word

1. favor
   flame
   fence
   frank
   flash
2. prime
   proof
   power
   paper
   purse
3. extra
   empty
   earth
   edict
   exact

Page 114, Trifles and Tangents

1. Only one: Ontario
2. Indiana, Idaho, Iowa, Illinois
3. Tennessee (eight) and Missouri (seven)
4. Nova Scotia (with New Brunswick); B.C. (with Alberta); and Newfoundland and Labrador (with Quebec)
5. Forty-eight
6. Nine
7. One: Saskatchewan
8. Four: New Mexico, Colorado, Utah, Wyoming
9. Nine: Maine, New Hampshire, Vermont, New York, Minnesota, North Dakota, Montana, Idaho, Washington. Michigan never actually touches Canada physically; yet parts of that state are north of Canada's border.
10. Three: Newfoundland, Nova Scotia, Prince Edward Island
11. Twenty-two: Alberta, British Columbia, Manitoba, Nova Scotia, Alabama, Alaska, Arizona, California, Florida, Georgia, Indiana, Iowa, Louisiana, Minnesota, Montana, Nebraska, Nevada, North Carolina, North Dakota, Oklahoma, South Carolina, South Dakota
12. *Alberta*, after daughter of Queen Victoria; *Georgia*, after George II
13. Six; seven if you count Nova Scotia: Newfoundland, New Brunswick, New Hampshire, New Jersey, New Mexico, New York
14. Prince Edward Island is way out in front with 18 letters. British Columbia is second with 15. There is a three-way tie for third: Massachusetts, North and South Carolina, each with 13.
    Although Canada owns the longest names, the United States has the corner on short ones: Iowa, Ohio and Utah have 4 letters. Quebec is the shortest Canadian one.

Page 115, In a Word

1. MAP, CHART
2. WONDER, AWE
3. SWING, PIGS
4. WAGER, BET
5. SCORE, TWENTY
6. STOP, HINDER
7. MAR, DEFACE
8. STRONG, FIRM
9. BAG, SACK
10. QUIET, STILL

Page 116, Visuthink

1.

•	•	•	•	×
•	•	•	×	•
•	•	×	•	•
•	×	•	•	•
×	•	•	•	•

2.

				•		•	•
•						•	×
		•	×				•
•		×		•			
			•		•	•	
	•			•	×		
	×		•		•		
×	•	•					

Page 120, Trifles and Tangents

1. True. It was German.
2. False. Custer's Crow scout Curley survived. (Custer's horse survived too; we thought we'd just throw that in—maybe you can use it sometime.)
3. True. He also wrote *The Charge of the Light Brigade*, an incident that occurred during the same battle and is more famous.
4. True. It's a pine tree.
5. False. It's scampo.
6. False. Eve Arden is her stage name. On the show she was Constance.
7. True. But if you said false, don't fret. His name was Albert Frederick Arthur George of Windsor, and he did not become Albert I because of a request of Queen Victoria that no kings ever be named Albert.
8. True.
9. True. And in 1939 as well!
10. True. In order, the top five are Smith, Johnson, Williams, Jones, Brown.
11. The volt in electricity is named after Count Alessandro Volta (1745–1827), an Italian physicist who devoted most of his energy to analyzing the composition of marsh gas. Later in life he turned to atmosphere electricity. Dieter Volt drives a bus in Stuttgart.
12. He designed the right arm, and the steel structure that holds it together.
13. Yes, and it's still in business: the Zion's Cooperative Mercantile Institution in Salt Lake City.
14. True. Not only the first woman, the first person. She did it successfully on October 24, 1901.

Page 123, In a Word

A perfect score, which may not agree with yours, is this one:

drop PLY — CANNOT
drop EAR — PARTLY
drop SUM — VERBAL
drop ICE — SUMMER
drop LAP — DIRECT
drop FEZ — PLURAL
drop LIP — FROZEN
drop ROE — POLICE
drop DIG — COVERT
BRIDGE

Page 125, Contemplator's Corner

1. This is such an oldie, we're not even going to tell you the answer.
2. The prisoners and guards.
   a. Guard and prisoner cross. Guard returns.
   b. Two prisoners cross. One returns.
   c. Two guards cross. Both get out. A prisoner returns.
   d. Two prisoners cross.